EAST-WEST and IS UNCLE JACK A CONFORMIST?

These two short plays by Andrey Amalrik are published to mark his arrival in the West after five years of imprisonment and exile in Siberia for writing 'anti-Soviet literature'. They are two of a group of plays written in the absurdist vein, whose charm and gentle satire have been somewhat overshadowed by the furore which greeted publication of his essay *Will the Soviet Union Survive until 1984?* As Amalrik says himself in a preface written specially for this edition of his plays, 'Above all I am a writer, a dramatist and a poet. Even my book *1984?* was originally conceived in order to vex the Soviet authorities as much as possible for refusing to allow publication of my poems and plays'. This volume offers a sample of Amalrik the dramatist in excellent translations by Daniel Weissbort.

In **East-West** a student and his mistress, a singer twice his age, arrive in a provincial town and take a grubby room in the only hotel. In it are three beds — the third is already let to a local Political Instructor. There follows a rapid succession of unmaskings, assassination and several mutual seductions. The whole play 'conceals some sharp political comment behind a romping exchange of partners' (*The Observer*).

Is Uncle Jack a Conformist? is a neat one-acter set in a Moscow flat where a diverse party are awaiting the arrival of Uncle Jack, the latest literary 'sensation'. Their pretensions are wickedly exposed as they anxiously discuss in advance what opinions they *ought* to be expressing about his work.

On its first performance in Britain, **East-West** was unanimously well received:

'A delightful satirical comedy whose nearest relative familiar to me is the characteristic Chekhov one-acter, only Amalrik is more sophisticated and — dare I say it? — funnier . . . The play is full of admirable dialogue, well translated by Daniel Weissbort. It kept me constantly amused, and seems to me admirable material for companies looking for fresh comedy with a contemporary flavour.'

The Financial Times

'It is an absurd satire, a dangerous calm on its surface, and reverberating with contempt for lives reduced to a series of reflexes . . . The bland display of so much emotional treachery and political desolation, with Moscow still the far away city, gives the sense of a rare voice finding a rare style.'

The Guardian

'. . . finely wrought political thinking and acute parody . . . Amalrik tears into the puritanism, the mis-information, the spy-phobia which official prying and revolutionary smugness foster.'

Time Out

'Most of all — remembering that the still young Amalrik has endured much hardship under the regime — I applaud the restraint, humour, and lack of malice of '

EAST ~ WEST & IS UNCLE JACK A CONFORMIST

Two Plays by
ANDREY AMALRIK

A Methuen New Theatrescript
Eyre Methuen · London

First published in Great Britain in 1976 by Eyre Methuen Ltd, 11 New Fetter Lane,
London EC4P 4EE
East-West and *Is Uncle Jack a Conformist?* copyright © 1970, 1976 by the
Alexander Herzen Foundation, Amstel 268, Amsterdam
'On Himself as a Playwright' and 'Postscript' copyright © 1976 by Andrey Amalrik
Introduction ('His Life and Writings') and English translation copyright © 1976 by
Daniel Weissbort
Printed in Great Britain by Expression Printers Ltd, London

ISBN 0 413 29390 4

ANDREY AMALRIK : I

His Life and Writings

In August 1971, Andrey Amalrik, sentenced under Article 190-1 of the Russian Criminal Code for circulating 'literature containing slanderous fabrications defaming the Soviet political and social system' was in the Kolyma forced labour camp (Magadan Region), 6000 miles from Moscow, serving three years of 'strict regime'. On his way to this camp he had collapsed with meningitis and been hospitalised in Novosibirsk where he nearly died. That Amalrik was aware of the grim implications of his non-conformist course can scarcely be doubted, and it is this awareness that underlines his joking, mocking, apparently almost light-hearted plays.

Paradoxically, these plays might be described as continuing in the nineteenth-century Russian realist tradition (that of Dostoyevsky, perhaps, rather than Tolstoy), whereas the socialist realists of the Soviet period have distorted and corrupted that tradition. The Theatre of the Absurd, as Martin Esslin says in his book of that name, forms 'part of the increasing endeavour of true artists of our time to breast the dead wall of complacency and automatism and to re-establish an awareness of man's situation when confronted with the ultimate reality of his condition'. In the case of Amalrik's plays, the political relevance is obvious, but, below the often almost topical surface, they too can be said to confront the ultimate reality of the human condition. Amalrik has chosen a most rigorous course, that of almost fanatical independence, and his dedication to the truth, however unpalatable or however dangerous, is, to a remarkable extent, exemplified in his life as well as in his writings. Though he himself adopts the characteristic anti-heroic posture of the post-war period, it is no less evident that he has followed in the heroic line of Russian radicals and non-conformists that begins with the Decembrists in the early nineteenth century and continues even through the black years of Stalinist repression. Despite his self-depreciating stance, his refusal to strike poses, his irony and coolness, Amalrik's own idealism cannot be doubted.

Andrey Amalrik was born in Moscow in 1938. When the Germans reached Moscow, his father was denounced and arrested for expressing the view that Stalin was to blame for the military catastrophe; he was sent to the terrible concentration camp on the island of Yagry in the White Sea, being released, however, at the time of the battle of Stalingrad, because of the shortage of officers. After the German bombardment of Moscow, Amalrik and his mother, for their part, were evacuated to the steppe town of Orenburg, returning only in 1943 to Moscow. Andrey's school career was a chequered one and he was finally expelled altogether, having to take his high school exams externally. In 1959 and 1962-3 he was a student in the Historical Faculty of Moscow University and was expelled from there too for his work 'The Normans and

Kievan Russia', which supported the so-called 'Norman Theory' of the origin of Kievan Russia — a theory that was considered to be insufficiently Marxist. It was this essay that was, in fact, the occasion for his first brush with the police, as he tried to get the Danish Embassy to forward it to a Danish professor of Slavic languages, not in itself illegal, but nevertheless intolerable to the authorities.

It was in 1963-64 that five of his seven plays were written. While looking after his father, who had been severely wounded by a mine in 1944 and further incapacitated by a series of strokes after the war, Amalrik evidently lived pretty well as he chose in Moscow, generally refusing to be inhibited by Soviet social and political conventions, taking a variety of temporary jobs, actively pursuing his interest in avant-garde painting, and meeting foreigners, including American diplomats and journalists who shared his interests. Indeed, according to Pavel Litvinov, he was the first dissident to engage in this practice. As early as 1963 the Moscow CID inquired into Amalrik's activities as an art collector and he was subsequently kept under surveillance, matters coming to a head in 1965 when he was arrested on a charge of 'parasitism', or failing to have regular employment.

The five plays, 'the writing of which', as he says, 'I regarded as my real job', were confiscated at this time, during a search conducted by the police while Amalrik was under preliminary detention. Amalrik's description of the search, the interrogations and the trial that followed reads like a scenario for an absurdist film, a sequence of dreams, nightmarish and comical, illogical though strangely inevitable, in which the actors, apart from the victim himself, appear to have only a remote or at best erratic understanding of the roles they are supposed to play. During the course of his investigation, Amalrik was questioned about the plays, the interrogator claiming that the illustrations (by Anatoly Zverev) which accompanied them were rather erotic. Much to Amalrik's surprise he did not seem particularly interested in the foreigners and, indeed, Amalrik was told at this point that he was being charged under Art. 228 of the Russian Criminal Code, i.e. with producing, harbouring and disseminating pornographic works: his plays 'besides being clearly anti-Soviet, are also of a pornographic nature, while the illustrations to them by Zverev are likewise obviously pornographic'. Amalrik, therefore, now found himself on a criminal charge and threatened not with deportation but with several years' forced labour. After a week's detention in prison, he was given a psychiatric examination, where, though he was again questioned about his plays, it transpired the interviewer had not even read them.

The following day, however, Amalrik was suddenly released and informed that his case hed been dropped by the MVD. He was told that the Moscow branch of the Union of Artists had decided Zverev's drawings were not pornographic, merely the work of a madman! The Union of Writers, for its part, had refused to give an opinion about the plays. An opinion given by Tatyana Sytin, literary consultant of the Lenin Komsomol Theatre, stated that she could not say whether the plays were porno-graphic or not, because she was not sure how to define pornography. The accusation of pornography was dropped and Amalrik reverted to his old status of 'parasite'. Nevertheless, in the trial that followed, the judge again spoke mainly about the plays, appearing less interested in whether Amalrik had been working or not. Behaving as a prosecuting attorney rather than a judge, he referred continually to the plays as anti-Soviet, Amalrik protesting that they were on the contrary Soviet, being written by a Soviet citizen and forming a part of Soviet literature. His sentence, ostensibly for 'parasitism', seemed, therefore, to Amalrik, more on account of the plays, which were central to the whole proceedings.

In his description of the drawn-out process leading to his arrest and trial, of the various interviews with officials and in particular of the trial itself, Amalrik paints a picture of a totalitarian structure that has, as it were, lost its nerve, that is in decline — 'the first such spectacle in history' as Max Hayward points out in his Foreword to *An Involuntary Journey to Siberia.* A curious spectacle is presented by the substitu- tion for the single godhead of a so-called collective leadership, a leadership that seems to have lost all sense of direction or purpose, that has inherited a massive bureau- cratic apparatus with all the means of coercion still at its command and yet is strangely incapable of investing this apparatus with anything more than a kind of automatic life. The subjects of this will-less and literally godless theocracy are, furthermore, as inert as their masters, conditioned to habits of absolute obedience, incapable of rebelling or dislodging the dead weight that oppresses them so monstrously.

The techniques of the Theatre of the Absurd are particularly appropriate in this real life situation. Popular culture, for example, against a background of impoverished linguistic and philosophical values resulting from the wholesale application of Marxism, allied to the devitalisation of Marxism itself, is specially vulnerable to an absurdist dramatic treatment; the general scepticism about language and, indeed, about what lies behind language is consistent with absurdist philosophy. Much of the 'fossilised debris of dead language', as Martin Esslin calls it, in the totalitarian states is still actively decaying, and Amalrik makes hilarious use in his plays of lists of clichés and slogans that, strung together in nonsense patterns, link the otherwise disparate and confused characters in a kind of conforming, mindless ritual. The dominating theme in his plays can be said to be confusion and disorientation. Amalrik strips off the social control to reveal the anger and frustration beneath. The inability of his characters to secure any gratification is striking, symbolised often by their sexual impotence or ambivalence. They pass the time in futile wrangling, usually at cross purposes with each other, faintly recalling the 'superfluous heroes' of nineteenth century Russian literature. Amalrik's concern with the violence of society, spreading from the top downwards, is much in evidence. The frustration, the social and political pressures, find their outlet in the search for scapegoats, as, for instance, in anti-semitism. The pervasive fear of authority, the cowardice of intellectuals, the mutual suspicions, lack of solidarity, tendency to select ritual victims to bear the burden of communal guilt — all these deeply-rooted social characteristics find symbolic expression in his plays. The absurdist vision has, indeed, become not only possible but almost mandatory.

In his theoretical writings, in particular *Will the Soviet Union Survive until 1984?* (which reached the West in 1969 and was very widely publicised, with its analysis of political feeling in the USSR as well as its spectacular predictions of a war between China and Russia and the disintegration of the Soviet empire), Amalrik demonstrated, besides cosiderable intellectual acumen, a striking independence of mind and spirit. His highly original critique is admirably balanced and sober, tolerant, scientific in the best sense. His writings, though not voluminous, range widely from documentation, as in *An Involuntary Journey to Siberia,* through social analysis and speculation, as in *Will the Soviet Union Survive until 1984?*, to the plays, in which potent images of the confusion and disintegration he sees around him are evoked and developed.

Yet, despite his sombre vision of Soviet society, despite his conclusion, based on experience in exile, that this society had lost the capacity for self-regeneration, Amalrik persisted, as a true absurdist, in defending democratic and libertarian values to the limit. In other words, he, in fact, refused to submit to pressures, to resign himself to a grumbling, but basically dishonourable, conformist existence. His own life, indeed, very properly confutes the cheerlessness of his views.

In July 1966 Amalrik was informed that the Russian Supreme Court had reversed the sentence passed on him by the lower court, and he returned to Moscow – an amazing reversal that lends further support to Amalrik's contention that the totalitarian state was not what it used to be, and that legalistic manipulation of it, as it were, could bear positive results in an indeterminate situation. Amalrik's lawyer told him of his meeting with the judge, where it became clear that the real reason for the sentence had been the plays, not the 'parasitism'.

Back in Moscow, Amalrik worked as a journalist specialising in theatre and the arts. He continued to pursue his independent, somewhat solitary, non-conformist course, in July 1968, for instance, picketing the British Embassy in Moscow in protest against arms being supplied to the Federal Government of Nigeria. At the end of 1968 the KGB forced the Novosti Press Agency, who had been employing him, to dispense with his services, and he subsequently found employment as a postman. His maverick temperament was further exemplified in his 'Open Letter to Anatoly Kuznetsov' in November 1969, in which he condemned the failure of intellectuals to preserve their 'inner freedom'. In his plays too, it is to be noted that he mocks the fatalistic intellectuals, prepared to compromise with repression and arbitrariness, basically impotent and contemptible as human beings. To quote from this letter: 'No form of coercion can be effective without those who are prepared to submit to it. Sometimes it seems to me that the "creative intelligentsia" in the Soviet Union, i.e. those people who are accustomed to think one thing, say another and do yet another, represent a phenomenon that is on the whole even more unpleasant than the regimes which engendered it.' But it was with the arrival and publication in the West in Autumn 1969 of *Will the Soviet Union Survive until 1984?* that pressure really began to build up against him and it became clear that he would finally be obliged to pay a heavy penalty for so blatantly offending against the canons of Soviet orthodoxy.

Amalrik was finally arrested in May 1970 and charged with circulating slanderous, anti-Soviet literature. He was taken to Sverdlovsk, no doubt to avoid the publicity of a trial in Moscow. Despite many appeals made on his behalf, including two applications by his wife Gyuzel to the USSR Procuracy, and a letter from sixty-four French historians to the president of the USSR Academy of Sciences, the trial took place in November 1970 and sentence was passed. He was accused specifically of writing and circulating *Will the Soviet Union Survive until 1984?, An Involuntary*

Journey to Siberia, A Letter to A. Kuznetosov and *Russian Painting in the Last Ten Years*; also of giving an interview to foreign correspondents. Amalrik refused to take part in his trial, instead submitting a note to the court in which he denied that his views were slanderous, stating furthermore: 'I also think that the truth or falseness of publicly expressed views can be ascertained by free and open discussion, but not by a judicial investigation' and referring to Art. 125 of the USSR Constitution and also to the Universal Declaration of Human Rights of which the USSR is a signatory.

When Amalrik was due for release in 1973, official reluctance to allow this irrepressible troublemaker loose led to new proceedings being instituted against him. He was given a further term of three years hard labour, whereupon he began a hunger strike, demanding that he be released. This hunger strike he maintained for 116 days and his sentence was commuted to one of three years exile. He and his wife lived in Magadan, where he, in fact, wrote another play and was given work in a local government office. Amalrik had never wanted to leave the Soviet Union, and when in 1976 he was given the opportunity of leaving on an Israeli visa, he refused on the grounds that he is not Jewish and that his wife, moreover, is a Moslem! However, conditions for him became increasingly difficult and finally he did agree to leave, arriving in Amsterdam in July 1976. His long-term plans at this point are uncertain.

Daniel Weissbort
August 1976

ANDREY AMALRIK : II

On Himself as a Playwright

In the event of some publishing house undertaking to bring out a collection of plays by a totally unknown author, and a foreigner as well, I should like to preface the book with a few words, to give the reader an idea of the sort of person he is dealing with.

I was born in Moscow in 1938. My earliest memory is of fear-distorted faces and a child wailing — a crowd, with me in my mother's arms, being herded into the metro. When the air-raid warning had sounded, we were in the street: the Germans were bombing Moscow. In fact, there was probably no need to herd anyone along; people ran for shelter of their own accord. My mother, however, says that I cried continuously in the metro and kept on repeating: 'They drove us like pigs, like pigs.' the next thing I remember is the oil-lit goods van in which we were evacuated, and the scorching steppe town of Orenburg, on the very frontiers of Europe and Asia. In 1943 we returned to Moscow. It was then that I realised there were two distinct periods of time: the one we were living in now, and a wonderful, strangely beautiful 'pre-war period'.

I was a very bad pupil at school and often played truant. I still consider those days I played truant as my best school days. Mother never tired of saying: 'If you go on like that you'll end up a herdsman.' Strangely enough her prediction came true: in 1965 I was sent to Siberia and tended cattle in the taiga pastures. Several times I was expelled from school for various periods, until I was expelled from the ninth grade altogether, taking my high school exams externally. I was twice expelled from Moscow University, too, where I studied Russian history. Up to university and after it, I engaged in a variety of occupations, mainly to earn some money. I worked as a cartographer, building labourer, press proof-reader, laboratory assistant in a medical institute, projectionist in news films, artist's model, translator, time-keeper at motor-racing competions, journalist, spent a short time in gaol, and in exile worked in a kolkhoz. It was at this time that I married Gyuzel, a Muscovite Tartar artist, who shared the hardships of my Siberian exile with me.

I wrote poetry from the age of nine, but at thirteen set up a puppet-theatre and wrote and staged plays with the assistance of two of my friends. Even earlier than this, musical comedy was a great theatrical experience for me. My aunt worked in it and I got to know both the good and bad sides of the theatre, thanks to which I learnt early on that art is relative. However, from about the age of fourteen, in an unconscious and afterwards conscious protest against the pseudo-art propagated in it, I hardly even went to the theatre. I started going only after I had returned from exile, in the line of duty, as I had to interview producers and stage artists; and I realised that a lot had changed for the better.

In 1962 I read a play of Khlebnikov's called *Mister Lenin*, and got the urge to write a play myself. I started writing it, but did not make much progress. A year later I chanced on someone's crude translation of Ionesco's *The Bald Prima Donna* — and was bowled over by it. Something I had only dimly perceived before, and that had appeared blasphemous to me, now seemed to take on a definite and harmonious shape. Practically the next day I started writing, and in three days finished a three-act play. It was a curious mixture of classical Russian drama and unassimilated absurdist devices. When I had written several other pieces and more or less knew what I was after, I returned to the first play and worked it over thoroughly, cutting it down to one act. Ionesco's influence was short-lived, like a shock: when *Rhinoceros* was translated, I was no longer particularly interested. For me, the second major revelation in contemporary drama was Beckett, in my view a master of perfect organisation. People who have read my plays have spoken of the influence of Camus and Sartre, but if so, the influence must be indirect, as, much to my shame, I am unfamiliar with their plays, just as I am with a great deal of what is currently happening in world drama. This is partly my own fault, partly the fault of those responsible for isolating Russian culture from world culture.

My favourite Russian playwrights are Gogol, Sukhovo-Kobylin and the little known Kharms, who derived to a considerable extent from Khlebnikov. They seem to have influenced me profoundly, but so probably have all the writers I have ever read, starting from the favourite of my youth, Blok, and ending with Chekhov, whose plays I always found tedious reading.

Of all the arts, I place painting first. I have been collecting pictures by young Russian artists — some of them friends of mine — for five years now. These people have shown an interest in what I write, whereas the few *writers* who were asked to read my plays have tactfully suggested that, at the best, it was graphomania, and at the worst, the ravings of a pathological maniac. Needless to say, I do not subscribe to this point of view.

Andrey Amalrik
July 1967
Makarovka

Postscript

During the nine years that have elapsed since I wrote the original short preface to my plays much has changed. From being an 'author known to nobody' I have become well-known, not, unfortunately, thanks to my plays, but thanks to a little book I wrote subsequently, *Will the Soviet Union Survive until 1984?* This has cast a strange light on all that I had written before, and my plays might now seem to be either the caprices of a political writer or else little more than literary illustrations of my political ideas.

In reality the situation is quite different. Above all, I am a writer, a dramatist and a poet. Even my book *1984?* was originally conceived in order to vex the Soviet authorities as much as possible for refusing to allow the publication of my poems and plays.

I believe the supposed political flavour of my plays has hindered their success in the West. I do not know whether many people have read them, but they have been performed very little. Another circumstance may also have played a part in this: when my plays reached the West a reaction against the avant-gardism of Ionesco and Beckett had already set in, and my plays were bound to be associated in the West with this tendency, in so far as the Russian traditions which had been my starting point are little known here. But the present dominance of naturalism in the theatre seems to me likely to be short-lived. I believe that the western theatre will soon turn away from the plays of Gorky and will show a new interest in Gogol, Sukhovo-Kobylin, Kharms and in my own work.

Andrey Amalrik
23 August 1976
Gruet

EAST~WEST

A dialogue in Suzdal

First presented by Theatre 84 at 84 Margaret Street, London W1 on 7 December 1971, with the following cast:

MANAGERESS	Lisa Hughes
MISTRESS	Constance Wake
STUDENT	David Leland
TSU SYAO, alias IVANOV	Jeremy Longhurst
GIRL	Petra Markham
OVERSEER	Malcolm Ingram

Directed by Doreen Cannon
Designed by Alain Courtney

The action of the play takes place in a Suzdal hotel over the course of a day. For the present purposes, I have disregarded the fact that there *is* no hotel in Suzdal.

Act One

A hotel room in the town of Suzdal. Three beds, a table, a clock, a wireless on the bedside table. The hands on the clock point to between one and two. The hotel manageress, an elderly women, has shown a STUDENT of about twenty and his ageing MISTRESS into the room. The latter have just arrived from Moscow.

MANAGERESS: Here's a nice little room for you.

MISTRESS: So I see.

MANAGERESS: And look at the view.

(The MISTRESS grunts.)

MANAGERESS: And the table-cloth — it was changed yesterday, you know.

MISTRESS: Really?

MANAGERESS: And the beds. (She sinks heavily onto a bed.) Soft and snug, you'll enjoy sleeping in them.

STUDENT: Do you like it here, my sweet?

MISTRESS: It's a grubby, miserable hole.

MANAGERESS (offended): What do you mean! You wouldn't find anything better in Vladimir even.

MISTRESS: All right. We'll take it. I'm so tired, I could sleep on a bed of nails. (To the MANAGERESS:) You know, we travelled all the way here from Moscow by bus with some young people, and not one of them offered us a seat.

MANAGERESS: I know — young people these days — they've no respect for their elders.

MISTRESS: That's not the point! It's just ordinary good manners to give up your seat to a lady.

MANAGERESS (eagerly): True. Our lot haven't got any manners. But I've heard there's a place called Leningrad where they always give up their seats. Of course, I can't say I've actually seen it for myself, but I've heard about it from reliable sources.

MISTRESS: I'm going to have a wash. I'm covered in dirt. I must look a sight. (She goes.)

MANAGERESS (to the STUDENT): Who is she — your mum?

STUDENT: No, she's my mistress.

MANAGERESS: Well, I hope you'll both be very happy.

STUDENT: Thanks.

MANAGERESS: And what are you?

STUDENT: I'm a student. I've come here to have a look at the old relics and monuments.

MANAGERESS: That's good. It must be interesting to learn how people lived in the olden days.

(The MISTRESS returns.)

STUDENT: I think I'll have a wash too. (He goes.)

MANAGERESS (to the MISTRESS): Who is he — your son?

MISTRESS (furiously): No, he's my lover!

MANAGERESS: Well, I hope you'll both be very happy.

MISTRESS (scornfully): Thanks.

MANAGERESS: And what are you?

MISTRESS: I'm a singer. I sing songs, you see.

MANAGERESS: Of course. That's a good occupation. Singing drives your cares away.

(The STUDENT returns.)

STUDENT: No-one could say you're too well equipped here.

MANAGERESS: Of course, you Moscow people wouldn't be used to the way we live.

MISTRESS: Do you have a restaurant in the hotel?

MANAGERESS: No restaurant. Words like that aren't even used round here.

MISTRESS: Where are we supposed to eat then?

MANAGERESS: We've got a dining-hall downstairs. But if you like I'll have a word with the girl and she'll bring your lunch and supper up. She works in the dining-hall and always brings the guests their meals in their rooms.

MISTRESS: All right. It's better than starving anyway. (Pause.) But what are three beds doing in the room?

MANAGERESS: There's another guest sleeping here – the political-instructor, Ivanov.

STUDENT: What do you mean? Surely there are some double-rooms?

MANAGERESS: What we haven't got, you can't have. But there's no need to lose your temper – he's a quiet man and you'll find you enjoy sharing with him. He's been staying here a long time and he gets his meals brought up too.

STUDENT: That's just marvellous – sleeping in the same room with a stranger!

MISTRESS: What's so terrible about it?

STUDENT: Maybe you'd like me to sleep with him?

MISTRESS: Please yourself.

STUDENT: Or maybe you'd like to?

MISTRESS: Why not?

MANAGERESS (sentimentally): Lovers' tiffs! I'll have a word with the girl now. (She goes.)

STUDENT: Why are you so bad-tempered?

MISTRESS: I'm tired. First the journey and then you dragging me round all those monasteries and churches. We haven't had a bite to eat since morning. And you'd drive anybody crazy with your stupid chatter.

STUDENT: What's so stupid about it? We don't yet know what sort of a man he is, and besides it's awkward sleeping three in a room.

MISTRESS: You're still full of petty bourgeois ideas.

STUDENT (put out): That's not what I meant at all. But what if he has sweaty feet? Just think of the smell!

MISTRESS: In a man that's not such a terrible fault.

STUDENT: And he probably snores at night.

MISTRESS: I know thousands of educated and interesting men who snore – I can't see any harm in it.

STUDENT: And I shouldn't be surprised if he drinks. There's no saying he won't come back at night dead drunk, cursing and swearing and vomiting all over the place.

MISTRESS: I've never known a man who didn't swear. And if he's sick, we can always ask the manageress for a basin.

STUDENT: But I've got a feeling he's probably a womanizer. He'll bring a girl back with him every night.

MISTRESS: What's so extraordinary about that! I never thought you'd turn out to have the morals of a reformed prostitute.

STUDENT: Don't be so crude! I'm going down to the post office. I must send a letter off.

MISTRESS: All right, goodbye.

(The STUDENT goes.)

(Alone:) To hell with him! (Pause.) Anyway, I must do my eyelashes. One's got to look after oneself.

(She attends to her eyelashes. Meanwhile a short, elderly man enters the room – the Political-Instructor IVANOV.)

IVANOV: Hello. I hope I'm not disturbing you?

MISTRESS: Not at all. You must be our room-mate?

IVANOV: Yes, I'm the Political-Instructor Ivanov. The manageress has already told me about you downstairs.

MISTRESS: I hope we all get on well together.

IVANOV: I'm sure we will. Are you staying long?

MISTRESS (coquettishly): No, a day or two at the most.

IVANOV: Lots of people come here in summer to see the local sights.

MISTRESS (continuing to attend to her eyelashes): To tell you the truth, it's rather a bore dragging round churches. I got covered in mud in some ruin.

IVANOV: I know — it's a disgrace. I've heard there's a government plan to pull down all the churches.

MISTRESS (examining her eyelashes in the mirror): It's high time.

IVANOV: What lovely long, silky eyelashes you've got.

MISTRESS: Do you think so?

IVANOV (thoughtfully): Yes. What's more you're an extremely handsome and well-built woman.

MISTRESS (laughs): You must be joking.

IVANOV (sadly): Joking's not my line. The plain fact, is I like you a great deal.

MISTRESS: I've heard that I don't know how many times . . .

IVANOV: I suppose you have. There's not much chance you'd fancy me — such a short, ugly fellow.

MISTRESS (quickly): A man doesn't have to be tall and handsome for me.

IVANOV (impressed): You're a remarkable woman!

MISTRESS: Am I?

IVANOV (looks at her): And you're so attractive — you've got such magnificent thighs. No man could resist you. Your friend must be very jealous of you.

MISTRESS (disparagingly): No, he doesn't appreciate me at all. I don't want to boast, but literally everywhere I go, I attract attention. Why, even today, while *he* was crawling about over his monastery walls, some man tried to get into conversation with me. He asked me the way to the woods. Of course, I didn't even know if there were any woods.

IVANOV: What was he like?

MISTRESS: Rather rough, but tall and interesting-looking, and he was wearing some kind of field-shirt.

IVANOV (jealously): He doesn't sound much cop to me. (Pause.) I'm not as young as I was and life's slipping by — I'd give anything to meet someone who had some real feeling for me.

MISTRESS: Real what?

IVANOV: Real understanding and feeling. I'd give anything to meet a woman who understood me.

MISTRESS: Well, there's no shortage of women. While we were out walking today, I counted eighteen women and only four men.

IVANOV (interested): Really? That's an important piece of statistical information. (He jots something down.) But those women aren't for me. There's only one woman in the world who can understand me.

MISTRESS: Really? Who is that?

IVANOV: She's in this room.

MISTRESS (looks round): I can't see her.

IVANOV: It's you.

MISTRESS (laughs): You must be joking.

IVANOV: I'm telling you, I can't live without you. Will you be my wife?

MISTRESS: Your wife — so soon. I've got to think it over.

IVANOV (urgently): I swear, I can't live without you. I'm already over fifty, it's time I thought about settling down to a happy married life.

MISTRESS: You're quite right. I'll not deny it — I'm no spring chicken myself. It's time to think about the future.

IVANOV: Exactly. I'm absolutely certain that we're meant for each other.

MISTRESS: All right then. In that case, I agree. (She kisses him.) But what do you think we should do now?

IVANOV (briskly): We can take a room here for the time being. I'm sick of this hotel. I think we must tell your friend right away.

MISTRESS (sadly): Poor boy. He's so much in love with me. He'll be heartbroken.

IVANOV (jealously): Not so heartbroken as all that.

MISTRESS: You don't understand. We're very much in love with each other. I'm even a bit scared to tell him.

IVANOV (gently): In the meantime, let's take a look at the little house we'll be living in, and then I'll come back here and have a talk with him myself.

(Enter the MANAGERESS.)

MANAGERESS: Ah, so you've already got acquainted.

IVANOV (dryly): Yes. What do you want?

MANAGERESS: Me? Nothing much — I just came to tell you that I've had a word with the girl, she'll be bringing your dinner up in a moment.

MISTRESS: Thank you. It's hardly likely we'd be having dinner right now.

IVANOV: We're going out.

MANAGERESS (to MISTRESS): Well, maybe your friend will want it?

MISTRESS: Maybe.

(IVANOV and the MISTRESS go.)

MANAGERESS (alone): Well, I don't know . . . First she wants dinner, then she doesn't want it. No good will come of it — no good at all. And then me dreaming last night I was a little girl walking in a graveyard picking flowers . . . It's a long time since I've had any dreams — six years or more.

(Enter the STUDENT.)

MANAGERESS: Your friend went out just a moment ago. She told me to tell you that she wouldn't be back for some time.

STUDENT: Really?

MANAGERESS: I don't get it myself. Will you be eating?

STUDENT: Yes, I'm famished.

MANAGERESS: Of course, you're young. The girl will be bringing it up straight away, I've already told her to. (Pause.) Your good lady didn't want anything to eat.

STUDENT: Well, I'm different.

MANAGERESS: Ha-ha-ha! Of course, it's nothing to do with me, but one can see you're not serious about her.

STUDENT: No?

MANAGERESS: You'll forgive me, but you're a young man and I'm an old woman.

STUDENT: Yes, I can see that.

MANAGERESS: You young people have your own ways: you come together, split up and no one gives a damn. It wasn't like that in the old days.

STUDENT: What was it like in the old days? I'm very interested in old customs as it happens.

MANAGERESS: In the old days there was one custom which was that you didn't leave your lawful husband. (Pause.) But of course there are all kinds of customs. I've heard there's a country called England where husbands and wives who have got divorced re-marry each other and live together again. It seems everyone does it there. Do you think that's possible?

STUDENT (considering it): I don't know. We don't know much about popular customs in other countries yet.

MISTRESS: No, me neither. It seems awfully strange though. (Pause.) I can see you've had a long walk today, you look tired.

STUDENT: Yes, we saw lots of things. I like it here. (The GIRL comes in. The STUDENT takes no notice of her.) There was one monastery in particular. It's an institution for young female offenders now, and they didn't want to let us in. But I begged them to and finally they did. Only they warned me not to talk to the girls. But while I was studying the paintings in one of the chapels completely on my own, a girl came in. She was wearing a torn jacket, her shoes were worn out and she had blue eyes, and she said 'hello' to me, and I said 'hello' back. And then another girl came in and said 'hello' — and I answered her. And then lots of girls came, and I greeted all of them politely, so that it completely took my mind off the paintings. But I don't regret it: they looked like bad nineteenth-century paintings. I haven't put it at all well, but the point is these girls were terribly moving. I don't really know why they all came to say hello to me. Perhaps it's just that they were happy some one was being friendly and polite.

MANAGERESS: But, then, you broke the rule about talking to them.

GIRL (interrupting her): I've brought your supper.

STUDENT: Oh, I didn't see you.

GIRL: Am I so inconspicuous?

STUDENT: Not at all.

MANAGERESS: Oh well . . . I've had a sit-down and one shouldn't overstay one's welcome. I'll be going, I've got a lot to do.

STUDENT: Come again.

MANAGERESS: I certainly will. (She goes.)

GIRL: Do you always want your dinner brought up at this time?

STUDENT: If it's convenient. But we're only here for two days.

GIRL: Oh. Well, I'll be back later for the plates. (She starts going out.)

STUDENT: Where are you going? Do sit down. Perhaps you'd take a bite with me?

GIRL (sits down): There's no need for that.

STUDENT: You're a very pretty girl. I'm very glad you came and that I saw you.

GIRL: Well, there'll be more opportunities to see me.

STUDENT: You've got lovely dark eyes and slender ankles.

GIRL (pleased): Really?

STUDENT: Yes. Do you live here?

GIRL: Yes. And where are you from?

STUDENT: I'm from Moscow. We just arrived today.

GIRL: You're new here then. You should be more careful.

STUDENT: Should I? Why, am I in some danger then?

GIRL: I'm not saying that, but it's better to keep your lips buttoned up.

STUDENT: Did I say something I

shouldn't have?

GIRL: You shouldn't have told the manageress about that conversation at the penal institution.

STUDENT: Why not? She seems like a pretty nice woman. She was talking about Leningrad as though it was Xanadu*.

GIRL: You're mistaken if that's what you think.

STUDENT: Really? Have you got something against her then?

GIRL: A lot more than you'd think.

STUDENT: What? Tell me.

GIRL: I've already told you more than I should have. (Pause.) And watch what you say to strangers.

STUDENT: But why?

GIRL: I can't tell you.

STUDENT: You shouldn't have told me anything then. I don't believe you.

GIRL: If you knew what I was, you'd believe me.

STUDENT: Who are you? (The GIRL is silent.) Come on, tell me – stop torturing me! Tell me what it's all about, or I'll do something silly.

GIRL: All right. I'll tell you. There's a Chinese spy called Tsu Syao in this town, and if you're not careful you might get mixed up in some nasty business.

STUDENT: How do you know about him?

GIRL: I'm one of his agents. (In despair:) I don't know why I'm telling you this – I'll do for myself.

STUDENT: Don't worry. I won't breathe a word about it.

GIRL: You won't?

STUDENT: No. You can rely on me. But how did you become his agent?

GIRL: He seduced me when I was still a very young girl and then he got me to work for him. But don't think too badly of him. He's not a bad old sort at all, and he doesn't have an easy time.

*Kitezh in Russian = fabled city.

STUDENT: How old were you when this happened?

GIRL: Seventeen. I'm twenty-two now.

STUDENT: How did he manage to seduce you?

GIRL: Curiosity simply got the better of me.

STUDENT: And was it nice?

GIRL: Yes. The only trouble is he hardly ever says anything.

STUDENT: Do you think one ought to?

GIRL (pulling a face at this flat joke): No, not actually during . . . But before and after. About two months ago there was a young mathematician from Moscow staying in the next room. He was very attractive and just before he left he took me into his room and told me all about how much his mother loved him and about all sorts of other joys of family life.

STUDENT: Before or after?

GIRL: Some of it before, but mostly after. (Pause.) But I don't think one ought to talk about such intimate matters.

STUDENT: Sorry. I won't ask you any more questions about it if that's how you feel. Tell me, is the manageress Tsu Syao's agent too?

GIRL: Quite the contrary. I think she's here to keep an eye on everyone.

STUDENT: How interesting. And do you work for the Chinese only?

GIRL: No. But don't tell anyone, I work for the Americans too. I was recruited by a C.I.A. man called Papayaki. He came to Suzdal disguised as an archaeologist.

STUDENT: That's a curious name — Papayaki. It doesn't sound English.

GIRL: He's Greek by nationality, but he was born in the United States. His parents emigrated there from Smirna.

STUDENT: How did he recruit you?

GIRL: He gave me a pair of stiletto heels. All I get is forty rubles and they cost forty-five. I wanted them so badly at the time, you know, every girl wants to be well-dressed. (Pause.) Do you think I'm a bad girl?

STUDENT: No. (Pause.) And what's he like, this Papayaki?

GIRL: Not much to look at, but he's so dynamic and full of fun. He's got very fat legs and his trousers hug them so tight that he looks like an Indian.

STUDENT: How do you know about Indians?

GIRL: What's so surprising about that? I was fascinated by ancient Indian literature while I was still at school. Have you read the *Mudrarakshasa* of Vishakhadatha, the son of the Maharajah of Bkhaskararadatha, grandson of Bamanta Bateshvarsdatta?

STUDENT: I have. And in case you don't believe me, listen: — The headman, Chandanadasa, the state criminal is being led off to execution accompanied by his wife and son. You ask, sirs, if there by any way in which he might gain his freedom? There is, sirs: if he delivers up the councillor Rakshasa's family. What is that you say? 'His love for the one who sought shelter in his house will not permit him to commit so base an act to save his own skin'. In that case, sirs, you may be assured of his blissful departure from the world. Of what use is your concern for his salvation now?

GIRL: Alas! Is there to be no distinction between scoundrels and innocent men? Dear friends, why do you now answer me not one word? Though, at such a time, it is scarcely surprising that you should fail to notice your friend standing close to you.

STUDENT (tearfully): Here is our dear friend. Turning away his grief-stricken face, his eyes clouded with much weeping, he gazed at me, the tears streaming down his face, though his body wishes to depart.

GIRL: Noble Chandanadasa, you have come to the place of execution. You have sent your people home.

STUDENT: Wife, return now with my son. It is not fitting that you should accompany me further.

GIRL (tearfully): But you are leaving for the other world, not for another country, my lord.

STUDENT: My lady, I shall die for another's sake, not on account of my own sins. Therefore do not grieve for me.

GIRL: My lord, even if that be so, now is not the time for a true wife to leave.

STUDENT: What therefore have you decided upon, my wife?

GIRL: I shall sanctify myself that I may follow in my husband's footsteps.

STUDENT: I had no idea you were so well-read.

GIRL: Hadn't you? You don't know me very well yet. Papayaki was surprised too: he thought I was just a simple girl at first.

STUDENT: Was he your lover too?

GIRL: You could hardly call him that. All he spent was one night with me.

STUDENT: How did he woo you?

GIRL: He fell on his knees and started kissing my legs.

STUDENT: Was he drunk? Perhaps he simply couldn't stand upright?

GIRL: Nonsense! It's just that he's very passionate, like all Greeks.

STUDENT: And what did you do all night?

GIRL: We discussed sexual perversions.

STUDENT: Was that so interesting?

GIRL: What are you smiling at? As it happens, he knows a great deal about it. For example he knows what exhibitionism is.

STUDENT: What is it?

GIRL: I don't know how to explain it.

STUDENT: What perversions does he suffer from himself?

GIRL: He didn't say. He's very secretive, like all secret agents. All he said was that he had a mistress in New York who turned out to be a lesbian. She works as an air-hostess. After he told me that, I started dreaming of . . . No, you wouldn't understand.

STUDENT: Why not?

GIRL: You're all the same, you men. You wouldn't understand how a girl could dream about anything else.

STUDENT: You're mistaken.

GIRL: All right, I'll tell you then; only, please don't laugh at me. I started dreaming of becoming an air-hostess and getting away from this damned town. (Pause.) Do you think I'm a stupid dreamy girl?

STUDENT: I think you're the most lovely woman in the world.

GIRL: Do you really?

STUDENT: Yes. You're the most lovely and the cleverest. (He tries to embrace her.)

GIRL: You mustn't. I've got to go. I'm already late for the dining-hall.

STUDENT: But we'll see each other again, won't we?

GIRL: All right.

STUDENT: When?

GIRL: I don't know.

STUDENT: This evening.

GIRL: All right. If you like, I'll come up this evening.

STUDENT: I'll come down with you now. I can't stand it in here anyway, so I'll go out for a walk.

GIRL: You mustn't. I'll leave on my own. Till this evening. (She goes.)

Curtain

Act Two

The same room. The hands of the clock point to between five and six. The Political-Instructor IVANOV is seated listening to the radio. Announcer's voice: ' . . . You have been listening to the news.' IVANOV switches off the radio. The STUDENT comes in.

STUDENT: Hello.

IVANOV: Good evening. You must be our new room-mate.

STUDENT: Yes. Are you the Political-Instructor Ivanov?

IVANOV: Himself. Very pleased to meet you. I think we'll get along together.

STUDENT: I hope so.

IVANOV: How do you like it here? Of course I'm a visitor myself, but I feel almost like a native.

STUDENT: Very much. At times I feel as though I'd been magically transported centuries back into the past. But I don't suppose you're interested in the past, and my passion for it must seem incomprehensible to you.

IVANOV: Not at all. Actually I think it's because of these lovely, unique old churches that I've stayed on here so long. Have you managed to see much yet?

STUDENT: Only in a very superficial way unfortunately. But I've managed to visit all the monasteries already.

IVANOV (surprised): All of them? There's a woman's penal institution in one of them, isn't there?

STUDENT: Yes. But they let us in.

IVANOV: How did you like the monastery?

STUDENT: To tell you the truth, I didn't really take it in properly. Don't misunderstand me, but those girls made me forget everything else.

IVANOV: I understand.

STUDENT: Of course, they were there for a good reason, but they had such childlike, innocent faces. They were digging some ditch outside. Their overseer struck me as a dreadfully unpleasant-looking man. He was tall, strongly built and wearing some sort of semi-military uniform. But the most dreadful thing about him was his face. That stupid, overbearing expression on it and the way he obviously revelled in his own power. I simply can't find words for it! People like that make me feel miserably helpless. It is a miserable feeling, isn't it?

IVANOV: I don't know.

STUDENT: But cathedrals make you forget all that. Or to be more precise, they create a world that seems to exist, as it were, in a dimension of time and space totally different to our own, so that you can't be in both of those worlds at the same time. Don't you agree?

IVANOV: I understand. Sometimes, when I'm looking at one of those churches or at the fading old frescoes, I feel strangely tormented. How can I put it? I begin to feel as though I lacked some vital organ to appreciate all this. Like Moses, I see the promised land but I cannot enter it. Does this mean anything to you?

STUDENT: Yes.

IVANOV: Maybe the feeling springs from an awareness of the impossibility of possessing anything. This is particularly true of ancient works of architecture. With a picture — or a reproduction of a picture — we can buy it — or contemplate buying it — and so always make the possibility — even if it is only apparent — of — sometime in the future — penetrating this picture — a permanent reality for ourselves — because this picture forms part of our property; to share its existence, becoming, as it were, the material out of which it is made, and the awareness of this possibility thus gives us the notion of sometime in the future possessing it, a notion that is not less precious in that, as time progresses, its realisation becomes more and more remote because even internally we can never possess these churches and convert their beauty into values that are more tangible for us. Do you agree?

STUDENT: I agree almost entirely.

IVANOV: So they live their own life and this clearly consists of self-contemplation, and for this reason there is no point of contact with them. O Suzdal. Sometimes I get the same feeling here as I got in Padua looking at the Giotto frescoes.

STUDENT: You've been to Italy?

IVANOV: Yes, on my way from Egypt. I was touring there and saw the famous pyramids.

STUDENT: Did you like them?

IVANOV: They're majestic structures. They were built by people with a hieroglyphic system of writing and dark skin.

STUDENT: You know, I can't get away from the feeling that there's some ambiguity, some *double-entendres* in our conversation. Now I know why it is. You won't be angry if I speak my mind will you?

IVANOV: Of course not. Go ahead.

STUDENT: Well. You are not the Political-Instructor Ivanov, you are Tsu Syao, China's man in Suzdal.

IVANOV: What makes you think that?

STUDENT: My conclusion is based on the deductive method.

IVANOV: I beg your pardon?

STUDENT: I once attended a meeting of political activists. They didn't talk about things the way you do.

TSU SYAO (overwhelmed by the STUDENT's logic): Yes, you are right: I *am* Tsu Syao. What do you propose to do?

STUDENT: Nothing at all. Everyone has the right to be what he wants to be.

TSU SYAO: In that case you shouldn't say my name out loud. Even the walls have got ears here.

STUDENT: I'm sorry, I didn't realise that.

TSU SYAO: All right, we'll drop the subject. (Pause.) I gather you've not come on your own?

STUDENT: No, I've come with my mistress, but she's disappeared somewhere.

TSU SYAO: I hear she's somewhat older than you.

STUDENT: Yes, twice as old at least.

TSU SYAO: It must be very interesting having a woman who is so much older. Unfortunately, that possibility no longer exists for me. (Pause.) Do you love her?

STUDENT: Yes.

TSU SYAO: How did you get to know her?

STUDENT: I met her at my grand-mother's the first time, and I was struck by her legs. In spite of every-thing, they didn't seem to join up under her skirt, but to divide some-where or other up there. That's what I mainly remember about her. Her legs never fascinated me as much again as they did that first evening.

TSU SYAO: And then you started an affair with her?

STUDENT: That was a bit later. It might even have been she who made the first move. Unfortunately, I'm usually very shy with women.

TSU SYAO: That sometimes disappears as you get older.

STUDENT: I hope so.

TSU SYAO: Only don't think that I'm talking to you as an older man to a younger.

STUDENT: Oh, I wasn't thinking that at all. The affair started two weeks later.

TSU SYAO: And then you were able to examine her legs?

STUDENT: Yes. Her legs — the legs of an ageing woman — always moved me a lot, especially because of the fine blue veins. I remember I used to switch the light on at night and look at her legs for a long time, and when this was no longer enough and a confused feeling swept over me — to relieve myself — I used to stroke her leg, starting from the tips of her toes right up to the top.

TSU SYAO: And what did you feel when you did that?

STUDENT: It's hard to explain.

TSU SYAO: And she didn't object to this pastime?

STUDENT: No, she simply went on sleeping. She's a terrible lie-abed. (Pause.) But of course I didn't touch her legs only.

TSU SYAO: What else did you do?

STUDENT: I touched her behind the ear.

TSU SYAO: And what did you feel when you did that?

STUDENT: Hardly anything. Then I stroked her cheek down to her chin.

TSU SYAO: And what did you feel then?

STUDENT: My hand felt an old woman's skin. Then I moved down to her neck and squeezed it slightly. She said: stop it, it's hurting me.

TSU SYAO: That's what she said?

STUDENT: Yes. Then I moved lower down and my hand, not stopping at the collar-bone, reached her breast.

TSU SYAO: And what did you feel then?

STUDENT: It was odd. But I went on and my hand moved over her belly, stopping at her navel.

TSU SYAO: And what did you feel then?

STUDENT: I can't explain it to you. Then I went on.

TSU SYAO: And what did you feel then?

STUDENT: It was very odd, quite unlike anything I've ever felt before. How can I describe it?

(A knock at the door.)

TSU SYAO and STUDENT (together): Who's there!?

(Enter a tall man in a semi-military uniform, carrying a sack. The OVERSEER.)

OVERSEER: Forgive the intrusion. I was passing by and thought I'd drop in. I hope it's not inconvenient.

TSU SYAO: Not at all. Of course not.

OVERSEER (sitting down): I know you, pop — you've been living here a long time. (To the STUDENT:) You're new though, aren't you?

STUDENT: Yes, I only just arrived today.

OVERSEER: Have you come to study our way of life, or are you just visiting?

STUDENT: I've come to study the monasteries. I'm a student.

OVERSEER: Ah . . . You were the one at the penal institution weren't you?

STUDENT: Yes. I was just saying what a deep impression your girls made on me.

OVERSEER: Of course, it's amusing for you visitors, but it's our work. I look at them in a different light now.

STUDENT: What are they in for? They looked between twelve and fifteen to me.

OVERSEER: Prostitution mainly. Some of those girls have been going with men since they were ten. We re-educate them here. An excursion to Moscow was organised for them, and not one wanted to go.

STUDENT: Really? Why's that?

OVERSEER: It's useless fussing over them. If it was up to me, I'd simply shoot all prostitutes like they do in China. Isn't that right, pop?

TSU SYAO: I think the Chinese are dealing with the problem in a formalistic, bureaucratic manner, substituting administration by injunction for real educative work.

OVERSEER: Perhaps, perhaps, I'm not saying they're not.

STUDENT: But with your views you shouldn't be in charge of those girls.

OVERSEER: It's easy for you to say what should and what shouldn't be. It's always easy to criticise from the sidelines. A writer once came here too, and afterwards he wrote that we didn't have any bread in Suzdal. So we haven't got any — so what! We haven't got any bread and all he's ever had is a load of intellectual junk. And he still gets published.

TSU SYAO: Well, if he does, it means that responsible colleagues regard him as publishable.

OVERSEER: Of course, of course, I'm not denying it. In the provinces we can't know all the facts. (Confidentially.) But I'm telling you, they don't know everything at the top either. Take brothels for example, they're forbidden in our country. So an important matter like that has been allowed to drift. Don't you agree young man?

STUDENT: I don't know.

OVERSEER: The important thing for us is strong family bonds. If we had brothels, there'd be no adultery, all this lying would stop, and most important of all, family bonds would be strengthened. So you see, we provincials know a thing or two as well.

STUDENT (to TSU SYAO): My friend's been rather a long time, I'll go down and have a look for her. (To the OVERSEER:) Goodbye.

OVERSEER: Be seeing you.

(The STUDENT goes.)

OVERSEER (critically): There's a young man with bees in his bonnet. That's what they teach 'em over there. But where do they get them all from? What's your opinion, pop?

TSU SYAO: I've not thought about it.

OVERSEER: So you don't know?

TSU SYAO: No.

OVERSEER (unexpectedly): Put your hands on the table! (He takes a tommy-gun out of the sack.) It's no use denying it. I know who you are.

TSU SYAO (his hands on the table): I'm the Political-Instructor Ivanov.

OVERSEER: You're Tsu Syao, the Chinese intelligence agent. I've had conclusive proof just today.

TSU SYAO: Yes, I am Tsu Syao.

OVERSEER (triumphantly): Comrade Tsu Syao, a full and complete confession will make it easier for you. Tell me: when did you start your espionage activities here?

TSU SYAO: In 1957.

OVERSEER (writing it down): Did you come here straight for China?

TSU SYAO: No, from Egypt. I was engaged on important work there on behalf of our leaders.

OVERSEER: Mohammed Salyam,

personal cook to Colonel Nasser — was that you?

TSU SYAO: Yes. But that job was too disturbing and I asked for a transfer to Suzdal.

OVERSEER: So you became the Political-Instructor Ivanov?

TSU SYAO: Yes. There was another idea, to send me to the State of Mississipi as a negro priest to organise sit-ins. What saved me was that I didn't know English.

OVERSEER: You've been working here for six years. Apart from circulating slanderous fabrications about the policy of peaceful co-existence, you have been recruiting agents. Tell me who they are.

TSU SYAO (eagerly): Two-hundred-and-twenty-five million Soviet people.

OVERSEER (writes it down): I see. (Briskly.) What are their names?

TSU SYAO (trying to remember): Aronov, Abarbarchuk, Abramovich, Abel, Avzelman, Arenson, Abakumov . . . I don't remember them all by heart.

OVERSEER: Where are the lists kept?

TSU SYAO: They're sent to Pekin.

OVERSEER: That makes it worse. The only thing that could help you would be for you fully to acknowledge the error of your dogmatic views and your dissident activity.

TSU SYAO: Never. He who fails to expose actions that are a betrayal of Marxism-Leninism and proletarian internationalism does not deserve the name of communist.

OVERSEER: Aren't you taking too much on yourself, interfering in our internal affairs?!

TSU SYAO (politely): Unfortunately, your statement is inconsistent, implausible, misses the point and in no way justifies my being interrogated.

OVERSEER: So you do not regard dogmatism as the main danger today?

TSU SYAO: The main danger comes

from the Yugoslav revisionists, who form the advance detachment of American imperialism.

OVERSEER (with hypocritical regret): Up till now we've had those kinds of speeches only from the most barefaced bourgeois obscurantists.

TSU SYAO: Down with revisionism!

OVERSEER (pointing his gun): If you don't change your mind, I'll fire!

TSU SYAO: The wind from the East will overcome the wind from the West!

OVERSEER: I'm going to shoot.

TSU SYAO: Shoot! Long live world revolution!

(A burst of fire. TSU SYAO falls. The MANAGERESS comes running in.)

MANAGERESS: Gracious! What did you do that to him for?

OVERSEER: He deserved it.

MANAGERESS: You've shot him dead! I thought you were just having a nice friendly peaceful chat together.

OVERSEER: He was an inveterate dogmatist. He had to be shut up — another moment and he would have said that we still had classes.

MANAGERESS (horrifed): God forbid! And he seemed such a nice man!

OVERSEER: They all *look* nice. (Briskly.) I will have to carry out a search. You will be the witness.

MANAGERESS: Of course. But why?

OVERSEER: The law says so. (He looks under TSU SYAO's pillow. Joyfully:) Here's material evidence: a copy of *The People's Daily* dated June 14 and a list of agents in Suzdal. What luck! tomorrow I'll kill the lot of them.

MANAGERESS: Well I never, well I . . . God only knows what's going on — and that's a fact.

OVERSEER (looking at the list): There's a lot of names here. There's even some hotel employees.

MANAGERESS (horrifed): Gracious! Who?!

OVERSEER: The girl who serves in the dining-hall.

MANAGERESS: The filthy little tramp! She was always in his room. And like a fool, I thought it was love. (Disparagingly.) Such a proud one too — sticking out her lips, never the first one to say hello.

OVERSEER (as a favour to the MANAGERESS): She'll be the first one on my list tomorrow. That boy who just went out seemed suspicious to me too. He's already broken a rule in the penal institution. What were they talking about before I came?

MANAGERESS: Oh no, that young man's nothing to do with it. They were talking about churches and their mistresses. He's a decent young fellow.

OVERSEER: What are you trying to defend anti-Soviet scum like him for? That's the way it all starts. One day he's having an orgy with his mistress and the next he's spying for the Chinese in Moscow.

MANAGERESS: No, I'm telling you, he's a decent young fellow.

OVERSEER: I can see you've got bees in your bonnet too. All right then — let him go back to Moscow. But if he asks where the Political-Instructor Ivanov is, tell him he's gone off to lecture the collective farmers on the international situation.

MANAGERESS: All right. But what shall we do with him?

OVERSEER: We'll stuff him straight in the sack — you drag him out to the cesspool and no-one will be the wiser. I'll lie in wait here in case anyone comes.

MANAGERESS: All right. But who's going to come?

OVERSEER: Maybe one of his agents. (They bundle TSU SYAO into the sack.)

MANAGERESS: What a weight he is! I don't think I'll be able to manage.

OVERSEER: You will. And if anyone asks you what it is, tell them it's food scraps for the pigs.

MANAGERESS: All right, I'll say it's for

the pigs. (Groaning, she drags the sack out of the room.)

OVERSEER (alone): I gave it him good, he didn't even have time to bat an eye lid. (Thoughtfully:) But it would take one more than a whole lifetime to mow down all the Chinese with a tommy-gun, there's so many of the buggers. Those up top ought to give that a thought too.

(There is the sound of footsteps coming down the corridor. The OVERSEER hides behind the night-table with his tommy-gun. Enter the Student's MISTRESS.)

MISTRESS: No-one here. Where could he have got to?

OVERSEER (creeping up behind her. Playfully): Bow-wow!

MISTRESS: Ay!!

OVERSEER (laughing boisterously): That gave you a good scare.

MISTRESS: It nearly scared me to death. Who are you anyway? What are you doing here?

OVERSEER: Don't you recognise me? I spoke to you in the monastery today, remember? You were with some young man then.

MISTRESS: Really? It's hard to remember everyone that speaks to me. But what are you doing here?

OVERSEER: I'm a friend of comrade Ivanov's.

MISTRESS: Oh . . . I was just looking for him.

OVERSEER: What do you want him for?

MISTRESS: That's none of your business! (Pause.) Actually, he and I are going to be married, but now he's disappeared.

OVERSEER: He said he'd marry you?

MISTRESS: Yes. So what?

OVERSEER: Nothing will come of it.

MISTRESS: Why?

OVERSEER: Comrade Ivanov doesn't exist.

MISTRESS: What do you mean, doesn't exist?! Only half an hour ago he was kissing me. Do you think I was kissing a ghost?

OVERSEER: No, I'm not saying that, that would be idealism. (Solemnly:) Did you know that Political-Instructor Ivanov is in actual fact the despicable Chinese spy and saboteur, Tsu Syao?

MISTRESS (astonished): No. I didn't know a thing about it.

OVERSEER (with determination): Why do you think he wanted to marry you?

MISTRESS (uncertainly): He fell in love with me. We were going to take a room together.

OVERSEER (solemnly): You simply fitted into his plan. He needed a secret address.

MISTRESS: But that's not what he told me.

OVERSEER (ironically): That's not what he told you! Do you really think the man in charge of Chinese espionage in a town like Suzdal has nothing better to do than tell you how much he loves you?! If you hadn't fitted into his plan, he'd have given you and all your romantic notions a kick up the arse instead. Yes, a kick up the arse and perhaps not just an imaginary one either.

MISTRESS (astonished): Is that right?

OVERSEER: What do you think! He might have seemed all right to you, but if you knew what I know about him, it would make your flesh creep.

MISTRESS: But I'd have been a good influence on him.

OVERSEER: Forget it. How could you influence him! He's a hardened spy. The best you could hope for would be to influence one of his insignificant agents. I'm afraid that it's he who would have a bad influence over you. He didn't suggest that you do some espionage work, did he?

MISTRESS: Oh no . . .

OVERSEER: You didn't give him any economic or political information, did you?

MISTRESS: Oh no . . . All I told him

was how a friend of mine deceived her husband — just by way of conversation, you know.

OVERSEER (indignantly): A fine conversation! So now the Chinese will be able to start saying that Soviet people are immoral!

MISTRESS (horrified): I never thought of that!

OVERSEER: You see. And here you are arguing with me . . .

MISTRESS (demure and coquettish at the same time): I'm not arguing . . .

OVERSEER (softening): Forget it all, then. You'd do better thinking about your own future.

MISTRESS (gently): Would I?

OVERSEER: You ought to link your destiny with someone more worthwhile.

MISTRESS (powdering her nose): But who?

OVERSEER: I'll be frank about it, what I felt for you in the monastery today is growing stronger and stronger.

MISTRESS (meekly): Really?

OVERSEER: Yes. It's just that I can't express myself, but my feelings speak for themselves. (He tries to embrace her.)

MISTRESS (backing away from him): But I can't marry you — after all I've already promised Tsu Syao.

OVERSEER (annoyed): Tsu Syao no longer exists: a revolutionary court has already imposed a penalty on him.

MISTRESS: That's different then. (Sadly:) Poor dear, he was so much in love with me. Do you love me? (The OVERSEER is so overcome by his passion for her that he cannot speak. The MISTRESS is convinced.) All right then, I agree.

OVERSEER: Hooray! (He tries to tumble her.)

MISTRESS: No, no! We must wait four years to make sure we really do love each other.

OVERSEER: That's too long. It'll kill me.

MISTRESS: In that case one day will do. Only let's get out of here: this place has too many painful memories for me.

OVERSEER: Let's go then.

MISTRESS: Wait. I'll leave a note for my former lover. Poor boy, he'll never forgive me. (She writes a note.) Here's what I've written: 'Farewell forever. Our ways are parting. Once I was yours, now I am nobody's . . . '

OVERSEER (jealously): Why nobody's?

MISTRESS: My god, you men are all so stupid when it comes to matters of the heart.

(They both go.)

Curtain

Act Three

The same room. The hands of the clock point to between nine and ten. The STUDENT is reading the note.

STUDENT: 'Farewell forever. Our ways are parting. Once I was yours, now I am nobody's . . . ' How idiotic! (A knock at the door.) Come in.

(The GIRL comes in.)

GIRL: Are you alone?

STUDENT: Yes. I'm very glad you've come.

GIRL: I've brought you supper.

STUDENT: Thanks.

GIRL: Sausages and macaroni. Do you like that?

STUDENT: No, especially not macaroni.

GIRL: Is that why you're so sad?

STUDENT: No. My mistress has left me. She was as fair as the rising sun.

GIRL: You mean that fat old thing you were with this morning?

STUDENT: Yes.

GIRL: A fine one to be sorry about!

STUDENT: Eh?

GIRL: She's got heavy, unharmonious features, expressionless eyes, and her hair's a mess.

STUDENT: Really? But she told me she had a lot of success with men.

GIRL: Who knows? It's possible. She's very clever — that might be why. The manageress told me that she was exceptionally clever. But not a bit good-looking. I'm very surprised at your taste. Have you always liked such hideous women?

STUDENT: I've only had one other woman before her.

GIRL: What was she like?

STUDENT: Repulsive.

GIRL: Why did you take up with her?

STUDENT: She was my school-teacher. I was in the tenth form and she taught us German. She was very plump and it was very pleasant squeezing her. She was very proud of this and was always saying that men fell into two categories: those that liked fat women and those that said they didn't like them.

GIRL: And what category did she put you in?

STUDENT: The second I suppose. She had a black moustache, shifty little dark eyes, and pimples on her chin and forehead. Her favourite writer was Heinrich Böll. However, I spent only one night with her.

GIRL: Very romantic, I must say.

STUDENT: Yes. And you don't know the most romantic part of it: when we kissed in the street.

GIRL: Who kissed who?

STUDENT: She kissed me. (Pause.) I bit her playfully in the breast, and she decided she couldn't allow her pupils such liberties. That was how our story ended.

GIRL: You tell it very movingly. Obviously you must have suffered a lot.

STUDENT: No. I felt nothing but disgust for her — I was so disgusted, my upper lip stuck out, and this lip was like a perpetual silent rebuke to her. Sometimes she'd notice it and say: 'Your

upper lip is exceptionally expressive.'

GIRL: So you have unpleasant memories of your school days?

STUDENT: Not altogether. That was when I was in the tenth form, but when I was in the eighth I fell in love with the canteen-girl.

GIRL: Was she fat too?

STUDENT: She was average. She had red cheeks, and she sold a watery kind of dish for breakfast in the school canteen. I can remember it had boiled beetroot in it. Do you like beetroot?

GIRL: No, do you?

STUDENT: I can't stand it. Well, one day, when the bell went and everyone rushed off to class, I stayed behind in the canteen with her and decided to have a go.

GIRL: Eat, or it will get cold.

STUDENT: I'm eating.

GIRL: What happened then?

STUDENT: Nothing much. I told her I loved her and couldn't live without her, and I put my arms round her. And she said: You'd better go — the head will be here any moment. Later I found out that the head was her lover. I was so embarrassed that I ran off immediately and never approached her again. But it left a great impression on me: ever since then I've been mad about girls who work in dining-halls and in food shops too, and at the same time I'm always terribly shy with them. I can't even conceive of an ordinary fellow like myself ever getting to be the lover of one of these wonderful creatures.

GIRL: Don't get upset. You're a pretty nice-looking boy, only you shouldn't cut your hair so short.

STUDENT: You think so?

GIRL: Yes. (Pause.) Was the canteen-girl your first love?

STUDENT: Yes. Without counting childhood loves.

GIRL: What happened when you were a child?

STUDENT: Nothing really. When I was

nine, I used to spend the winter in the country with an old Lettish woman. Anyway, one day her twelve-year old grand-daughter slipped into my bed. I was very scared and couldn't understand what she wanted. Well, her grandmother woke up and rescued me and gave her a good hiding. I didn't like her a bit anyway. Her hair was cropped and she looked like an urchin. I'd rather have made love to her sister. She was nineteen, with a big bosom, and her presence always stirred me up.

GIRL: You say that you were totally ignorant?

STUDENT: That's right. But I was always attracted to women. I remember that when I was only five, women already occupied my thoughts. For some reason, as a child, I was always imagining naked women, and as I was completely ignorant about the female anatomy, the means of satisfaction, as I'd call them now, were somehow linked in my mind with the female heel, with touching women's heels. I don't know why myself. And years later, when I'd completely forgotten all this, the word 'heel' seemed somehow terribly indecent to me — I couldn't say it out loud and when I heard it in conversation or came across it in a book, it gave me a shock and made me feel embarrassed. And though I completely forgot these infantile fantasies in youth, I was always excited by the thought that sometime or other I might touch a woman's heel.

GIRL: And did you?

STUDENT: For some reason, I didn't. I simply forgot about it with the school-teacher and later the heel somehow no longer attracted me.

GIRL: And what were your feelings the first time you went with the school-teacher?

STUDENT: It's hard to say. It reminded me a lot of the dreams I dreamt when I was about fourteen. What did you feel the first time?

GIRL: It hurt me. And it disgusted me. Please don't ask me about it. I can't

speak about it like you can. (Pause.) There was even an occasion before then when I was a child, the first time I came up against, well you know what . . .

STUDENT: What happened?

GIRL: Don't you tell anyone. I was about twelve at the time, I was picking flowers in a graveyard and suddenly I heard someone saying: 'Darling . . . darling . . . ' And there was this man coming towards me out of the bushes with his arms stretched out in front of him. He was elderly and stark naked, but he moved very slowly and kept on pleading: 'Darling . . . darling . . . ' I was so scared that I couldn't move at first, and he kept on coming. But as he was moving so slowly, I picked up my scattered flowers, slowly too, got up and only then started running. I ran and ran — I felt as though he was chasing me and was going to catch me up though he didn't even try to. A bit further on, I ran into some people and burst out crying — I was so upset, but all I said was that the graveyard had scared me and I stuck with them as I was frightened of being on my own. (Pause.) After that I sometimes dreamt . . . but don't start getting any ideas about me . . . afterwards I sometimes dreamt that that man, naked I think, was taking me in his arms and kissing me. It's horrible, isn't it?

STUDENT: I don't know.

GIRL: And what kinds of dreams were you saying you dreamt when you were fourteen?

STUDENT: Well, I think the usual sorts of dreams kids of that age dream. Later on, when I was about eighteen, I got very interested in dreams and trained myself to analyse mine while I was actually dreaming them, and often worked out what they meant and why I was dreaming. I didn't always manage to do this, mind you. Once I dreamt that I came face to face with a woman in a long, narrow corridor, put my arms round her and grabbed her by the breast. This made me realise that it was all a dream — that was why

I was being so daring with her — but if it was a dream I thought, then it must mean that what I was squeezing wasn't a woman's breast but something else. Curiosity made me sacrifice the satisfaction I was getting from squeezing the woman's breast and try to wake up and see what it was in real life. I woke up and saw that what I was embracing was a bicycle frame.

GIRL: A bicycle frame?

STUDENT: Yes. But of course, this was simply the dream continuing. One can wake up that way in dreams several times: it's really just one dream following another.

GIRL: I have dreams too. Maybe I'll tell you about them . . . later. (Pause.) But tell me, has there ever been any really great love in your life?

STUDENT (thinking): Once, possibly. I saw a girl in the cinema and was bowled over by her. She scarcely came up to my shoulders, she had a large behind and short podgy legs, and a little snub-nose in front and dull blue eyes. I didn't see what her hair was like. After the film I followed her out and trailed her for a long time without being able to bring myself to speak to her. My mouth was all dry with excitement.

GIRL (ecstatically): Oh, you're so passionate! But did you speak to her in the end?

STUDENT: Yes. She turned out to be nineteen-years-old and was working as a draftswoman. But she wouldn't let me make a date with her. She said she had a young man. That excuse surprised me but I let her be.

GIRL (disappointed): You were only infatuated in that case. If you'd really been in love you wouldn't have let it go at that.

STUDENT: Maybe. I'm often running across women in the street who appeal to me.

GIRL: And do you try to get to know all of them?

STUDENT: Of course not. Usually I can't even bring myself to approach them, which is why each one seems to me like the one I could be happy with. But as this is what I think each time I see a fair stranger, it's obvious that there are going to be many more such encounters in the future, and that helps me reconcile myself to my loss in each particular case.

GIRL (clearing away the plates): Well, I'll be going.

STUDENT: Where are you off to? Didn't we agree to meet this evening?

GIRL (uncertainly): I've got to clear away the plates in the dining-hall.

STUDENT: I won't let you go anywhere.

GIRL: Won't you? Why not?

STUDENT: Because I love you. (He embraces her.)

GIRL: That's what you tell all the girls, I bet.

STUDENT: No, only you. Do you like me?

GIRL: I don't know.

STUDENT: You have beautiful slender hands and long silky eyelashes. Thy hair is as a flock of goats, that appear from a mount Gilead, and thy belly is like a round goblet which wanteth not spiced wine.

GIRL: What strange words. Go on.

STUDENT: I have compared thee, O my love, to a company of horses in Pharaoh's chariots . . . I can't remember any more.

GIRL: You didn't make it up yourself?

STUDENT: No.

GIRL: I thought it was you.

STUDENT: Some of it was me. The main part. Do you believe me?

GIRL: I don't know. (Pause.) You know, I'm desperate to get away from here. It doesn't matter where — just go get away. I simply can't stand it here — sometimes I even cry at night.

STUDENT: My love, my poor sweet. We will leave.

GIRL: Will we?

STUDENT: Yes, we'll leave together.

GIRL: How wonderful! Where shall we go?

STUDENT: To Leningrad or Moscow, if you like.

GIRL: That would be interesting. I've never been there.

STUDENT: Or we could go to Tallin. In the old town the streets are so narrow, if you stand on one side you can touch the house on the other.

GIRL (dreamily): We'll go there.

STUDENT: And there we'll get on board a great white steamer and sail to London. In London there's a famous clock on the houses of parliament. It's called Big Ben.

GIRL (dreamily): Big Ben . . . Those words leave a taste on my lips as if my beloved had kissed me.

STUDENT: And then we'll hitch lifts in lorries and travel round England. English lorry drivers are very sociable — they give their passengers biscuits and tell them all about their children, wives and mistresses and about how they deceive their wives on long trips.

GIRL: Will we tour the whole of England?

STUDENT: Yes. And then we'll board an aeroplane and fly westwards, and after a few hours we'll see a vast, wonderful country below, with blue lakes to the north and broad rivers flowing towards the south. And we'll ask: What country is this? — and the air-hostess will answer: It's America. Do you remember how you dreamt of becoming an air-hostess?

GIRL (dreamily): Yes . . . And what will happen next.

STUDENT: Then we'll travel around a great deal, from New York to Los Angeles and from Oregon to Miami, and no-one will ever make us feel strangers in that country.

GIRL: How wonderful that would be. You know what — only don't be angry — let's take Tsu Syao with us.

STUDENT: Tsu Syao?

GIRL: Yes. But don't misunderstand me — he was almost like a father to me.

Anyway he's a lot older than me. Sometimes, when I was frightened and cried, he would stroke my hair and say: 'Don't cry, little Russian girl, it hurts me when you cry.' He's so simple-hearted, so naive and he dreams of marrying some fat Russian woman. He'd like her to be elderly and a good housewife. But he's a very entertaining man and very kind. Once he told me several stories. Do you know the Chinese stories about wolves?

STUDENT: No.

GIRL: Oh, they're fascinating. They're about werewolves actually who take on human shape and sometimes live among human beings for ages, get married and raise a family, and also there are wolves disguised as scholars who display remarkable erudition. Their wolflike nature reveals itself only in dreams or in the presence of dogs. If you like, I'll tell you something about them.

STUDENT: Go ahead.

GIRL: Only, I don't remember all the details. Well, never mind, listen. In the days of Chen-yuan, the ten-year-old son of the district official Bei, formerly from Tsianlin, fell seriously ill. He was intelligent and educated and of refined appearance. Bei sought the monk Daos who might cure his son with incantations. Then one day someone knocked at the gate declaring that his name was Gao and that he was a scholar, and explained that his business was incantations. Bei at once invited him in and he began to treat the boy. The latter improved but did not recover completely and Gao came each day. Then one day another scholar, Van, came and declared that he possessed secret powers and could drive away devilish ailments, and wished to see the child. Bei showed him his son, and Van, horrified, said: 'This boy's sickness comes from the wolves. It'll soon be too late to cure him.' Bei at once told him about the scholar Gao. Van began to laugh and said: 'How do you know that this Gao is not himself a wolf?' At this moment Gao happened to come in and started swearing: 'Who summoned this wolf to the house!' 'I see! So this evil wolf just happens to come today!' cried Van furiously. Bei was thunder-struck. At this moment a certain monk appeared and asked to be received. Scarcely had the two scholars seen the monk than they began to abuse him violently, saying how dare this wolf pass himself off as a monk and deceive people! He for his part started cursing them, shut the door at once and began to struggle with them. Bei was scared out of his wits. Only towards evening, when everything had calmed down, did he open the door; he saw three dead wolves lying there. His son recovered the next month.

STUDENT: What's the story called?

GIRL: 'Wolves fall out'. Did you like it?

STUDENT: Yes. Do you know any other ones?

GIRL: I know one more story, only it's a very sad one.

STUDENT: Please tell me it.

GIRL: It's called 'The Beautiful Zhen'. (She mimes the story.) This took place in the ninth year of the Celestial Jewel. There were two friends; In, the ninth in his family, and Chen, the sixth; they used to carouse and debauch together although In was very rich and Chen very poor. Once they were on their way to a house of ill-fame when Chen said: 'I have business in this neigh-bourhood; I shall come on later'. But when Chen had left the spot — he was mounted on an ass — he saw an extraordinarily lovely girl who was walking along accompanied by two women, her servants. He followed her for a long time not daring to speak. but the girl looked at him and encouraged him, and finally he plucked up his courage and said: 'How is it that so lovely a one as you is travelling on foot?' She answered him and he offered her his ass, and thus they proceeded, talking and touching each other until they grew completely shameless. They came to this girl's home — she lived in a palace — and passed a wonderful night there. Chen left the palace towards morning, and when he returned later found only ancient ruins. A merchant he met told him that a young she-wolf lived here, who often enticed lovers to her side, and he realised that he had been with a she-wolf.

STUDENT: Is that all?

GIRL: No. Listen what happened next. In reproached Chen for not coming, but Chen told him nothing. And then one day at the market he saw this girl again. She covered her face with her hands and tried to escape but Chen overtook her and asked her why she was running away. 'But you know who I am,' she answered, 'it must be terribly humiliating'. Chen swore to her that it was not humiliating and begged her to become his wife. She was overjoyed and agreed. Then Chen came to In and told him that he was marrying a girl of exceptional beauty and asked him for pillows and a bedspread, as he himself possessed nothing. 'I suppose this beauty of yours is some hideous creature', said In, but he gave Chen everything he asked for, as they were friends. Later he sent his servant to inspect Chen's wife. The servant returned and said that she was the most beautiful of women, far more beautiful than any In knew. When In heard this he went to her in Chen's absence and tried to seduce her. And as she refused him, he tried to over-come her by force, whereupon she said: Very well, I consent', so that he would let her go. This was repeated six times. And when she felt the strength ebbing from her, she said: 'I consent, but I feel sorry for Chen'. 'Why?' said In. 'He is strong and tall, but he cannot protect his wife, because he lives in your house, wears your clothing and bears your weapons'. Then In said, 'I dare not do it', and left, for he was a knight and an honourable man. After, Zhen and Chen lived together a long time and In loved her and brought her clothes and Zhen found him beautiful women from among the wolves and the daughters of men.

STUDENT: Is that the whole story?

GIRL: No. Chen entered public service and on one occasion had to go to a distant province for a month. He wanted to take Zhen with him, but the latter refused. 'A fortune-teller prophesied that I would die on a journey', she said, but Chen said: 'What nonsense!' and insisted that she came. On the way they chanced upon a large hunt with dogs. Before Chen could collect himself, Zhen had leapt from her horse, changed into a wolf and was trying to escape the dogs which set off in pursuit of her. Chen galloped after them and tried to head the dogs off, but they swiftly overtook her and tore her to pieces. Chen bought her remains from the hunters and buried them. When, on his return, In asked him where Zhen was, Chen answered that she had been torn to pieces by dogs on the journey. 'Dogs may be savage creatures but they never do that to human beings', answered In, and then Chen told him that Zhen was a wolf. In wept bitterly, and they both went to her grave. She was a remarkable wolf: generally wolves do not like men and do them harm. But Chen loved her beauty and did not concern himself with her soul. Subsequently he was appointed army-inspector. He became very rich and kept more than ten horses in his stables. He died at the age of sixty-five. In survived him and told this story.

STUDENT: So this is all true?

GIRL: Of course. Tsu Syao knows many stories like it. He knows all the stories of the Tang period collected by Li Fan in the Tai-pinguan-tsi collection. It comprises fifty volumes.

STUDENT: All of them about wolves.

GIRL: No, only ten of them about wolves, and forty about demons. The collection is divided into a number of sections. The first is called The Immortals.

STUDENT: And the second?

GIRL: Fairies, followed by Magic.

STUDENT: Then Sorcerers.

GIRL: Next, Strange People.

STUDENT: Unusual Monks.

GIRL: Buddhist Hermits.

STUDENT: Retributions, Omens, Prophesies.

GIRL: Rewards and Punishments.

STUDENT: Oracles.

GIRL: Famous Wise Men.

STUDENT: Unselfishness, Courage.

GIRL: People of Understanding.

STUDENT: Investigation, Ability.

GIRL: Clever People, People of Talent, Scholars.

STUDENT: Elected Representatives, Officials, Dignitaries, Military Leaders.

GIRL: Heroes, Knights.

STUDENT: Nature, Works, Fame, Confucianism.

GIRL: Music, Writing, Painting, Calculation.

STUDENT: Divination, Doctoring, Physiognomy.

GIRL: Dexterity, Theatre, Utensils, Wine, Food.

STUDENT: Friendship, Extravagance, Cunning, Flattery, Mistakes.

GIRL: System, Haste, Jokes, Laughter.

STUDENT: Uncouthness, Imperturbability, Arrogance, Cruelty.

GIRL: Women, Feelings, Man-servants and Maid-servants.

STUDENT: Dreams, Fortune-telling, Wizardry, Witchcraft.

GIRL: Gods, Devils, Demons, The Soul.

STUDENT: Devilry, Ghosts, The Supernatural, Reincarnation.

GIRL: Recollection of Previous Incarnations.

STUDENT: Graveyards, Epitaphs.

GIRL: Thunder, Rain, Mountains, Rocks, Waters, Jewels.

STUDENT: Plants, Dragons, Tigers, Domestic Animals.

GIRL: Foxes, Snakes, Birds, Water Creatures, Insects, Barbarians.

HOSTESS: Wonderful! Nothing straight out, yet it manages to hit the nail on the head. Most daring.

LADY: Yes, and so lyrical too. Not the usual tripe we get masquerading as poetry. Why, only yesterday, I saw this bit of rubbish in the *Literary Gazette*:

We are the wolf's offspring.
We don't live in the woods for nothing!

HOSTESS: Frightful!

JOURNALIST (his interest aroused): Very interesting.

CRITIC (to the LADY): But in what way are these lines any different from the ones we've just heard. It's true that, at first glance, 'The Ass and the Victim' seems more modern, but if you consider a bit closer, you find the same obsolete cadences reminiscent of Blok.

LADY (taking offence): Why say that! In the first place, Blok's not in the least obsolete, and secondly, if we're to speak about traditions, the poet isn't taking after Blok here, but Pushkin.

SON: I'd say Lermontov.

DAUGHTER: And I'd say Nekrasov.

HOSTESS (politely): Well, Russian poetry anyway.

GUEST (in undertone to the DAUGHTER): Whose play?

DAUGHTER (patronisingly): Uncle Jack's.

HOSTESS (politely to the LT.-COLONEL): And what did you think of it — did you like the poem?

LT.-COLONEL (shyly): What I liked about it was the keen sense of civic responsibility displayed. I myself was a victim of injustice in the days of the cult.

CRITIC: I'm not saying the poem hasn't got its good points, but that's all by the way. It's a striving after poetry, but it's not poetry yet. (To the SON:) What sort of a man is he? Is he published?

SON: No, he's a formalist, so he's not published.

LADY: What does he live on?

SON: Friends help him out. He's got lots of friends, five hundred, maybe even a thousand.

LADY (enraptured): A thousand?! That's almost a million!

SON (modestly): Yes, almost.

CRITIC (critically): All the same, a thousand is less than a million.

SON (displeased): Yes, a bit less.

HOSTESS (sadly): Poor boy though — it must be very hard eating out at strangers all the time. It doesn't take long to ruin your digestion.

SON: His digestion's completely ruined already.

DAUGHTER: And his heart and lungs.

SON: And kidneys and liver.

HOSTESS: How terrible!

JOURNALIST (his interest aroused): Very interesting.

GUEST (in an undertone to the DAUGHTER): And who is Uncle Jack?

DAUGHTER (without condescension): Uncle Jack is Uncle Jack. (The GUEST retires into his shell, mortified.)

LADY: I was recently told an infallible method of ensuring good health. I simply must pass it on to you.

HOSTESS (politely): How interesting! Please do.

LADY: It's quite simple really. You breathe in through your nose and hold your breath, letting your stomach out and keeping your mouth shut. That's the real secret of good health; it's the system of Comrade Ivanov, works superintendent at the building department. This secret was told to me on the 26th of February by my neighbours.

DAUGHTER: Comrade Petrov's system is far more sensible. It's to do with the free movement of all parts of the body — arms, legs and trunk. You walk in a straight line, tossing your head like a horse.

SON: The way I see it, if you want to be healthy you must follow Comrade Sidorov's system. Keep your head straight, turn it as little as possible to right or left and squint sideways if you have to.

CRITIC: I think the soundest system is Comrade Semyonov's. Your eyes meet when you bump into someone and then electricity is wasted, so the idea is to keep them fixed on the level of people's mouths.

LT.-COLONEL (shyly): Excuse me, but in that case why don't animals possess intellect.

CRITIC: Because all their magnetism goes into their muscles.

LT.-COLONEL: And why do they walk in a horizontal position?

CRITIC: Because, when the head is lowered, the mouth closes, and when the head is raised, the mouth opens, which proves that Comrade Semyonov's system is correct.

LT.-COLONEL: And could you tell me something else. Can an ordinary Soviet citizen write a letter to the President of the United States?

CRITIC (guardedly): Why do you want to know?

LT.-COLONEL (with hope in his voice): Maybe the swine can be persuaded to stop the bombing.

HOSTESS (tentatively): That's the yogis' system, isn't it?

JOURNALIST (his interest aroused): Very interesting.

DAUGHTER: I've heard Uncle Jack is studying yoga.

CRITIC (identifying proudly with Uncle Jack): He even advocates it, in spite of everything in his latest play.

DAUGHTER: Is that the one he's going to read today.

CRITIC (proudly): I imagine so.

HOSTESS (politely): Perhaps you'd give us a short summary of it, otherwise we mightn't understand a thing, Uncle Jack being so inarticulate

LT.-COLONEL (shyly): I won't

understand.

LADY: I won't understand either.

SON: I won't understand at all.

CRITIC: I'd be glad to. The play is called 'Tsirlin and Tsipelzon, or the apotheosis of good'. (A murmur of excitement.) Act one: Tsirlin rapes Tsipelzon.

ALL: Oh!

CRITIC: Act two: Tsipelzon rapes Tsirlin.

ALL: O-oh!!

CRITIC: Act three: Tsirlin and Tsipelzon rape each other.

ALL: O-o-oh!!!

CRITIC (triumphantly): Act four: Ivan Ivanovich arse moves to a new workers' block.

(Silence.)

HOSTESS: It's most daring. Nothing straight out, yet it manages to hit the nail on the head. I think it's superb.

LADY: Yes, from a social point of view the play can't be faulted. The only thing is, it's pointless using expressions like 'arse'. In the twenties it might have seemed very new and daring, but nowadays it just looks like obscenity for its own sake.

SON: In my opinion, 'arse' is very much to the point here and carries considerable semantic weight. But as regards the social aspect, don't you feel that at the end of the play the author is compromising with what he starts off by attacking, and is trying to get round the authorities by tacking on a happy ending — this move to a new flat — so that they should let the rest pass?

CRITIC: I totally disagree with you. You've completely missed the irony of it. As it happens, that's the best part of the play.

DAUGHTER: What's so good about it! He's simply being obsequious and trying to show that people are well off in our country, as they get new flats.

LADY: But you've all got it wrong! On the contrary, what he's trying to say is that the new flats are in no way better than the old ones, but even worse.

SON: All the same, the author is showing a tendency to conformism.

CRITIC: Not in the least! He's a regular non-conformist.

SON (aggressively to the CRITIC): I assure you, he's a conformist.

CRITIC (aggressively to the SON): And I'm telling you he's a non-conformist.

SON: A conformist, a conformist!

CRITIC: A non-conformist, a non-conformist!

SON (furiously): A conformist!

CRITIC (furiously): A non-conformist!

HOSTESS (politely to the LT.-COLONEL): And what did you think of it — did you like the play?

LT.-COLONEL (shyly): What I liked about it was that the end was optimistic. I myself am shortly moving to a new flat.

SON: I'm not saying the play hasn't got its points, but from a purely literary point of view it's very old fashioned. At first glance it seems to be in the tradition of the absurd, almost like Ionesco, but on closer examination, it's just Ostrovsky updated a little.

CRITIC: That's simply ridiculous. There's not a trace of Ostrovsky there. Now Gogol — that's another matter.

LADY: I'd say Sukhovo-Kobylin.

DAUGHTER: And I'd say Saltykov-Shchedrin.

JOURNALIST (to the LT.-COLONEL): Where are you moving to then?

HOSTESS (wanting to make her own contribution to the literary discussion): Which Ostrovsky did you have in mind — Aleksandr Nikolayevich or Nikolai Aleksandrovich?

SON: Aleksandr Nikolayevich.

CRITIC: Nikolai Aleksandrovich.

SON (to the CRITIC): Excuse me, but what's Nikolai Aleksandrovich got to do with it?

CRITIC (to the SON): And what's Aleksandr Nikolayevich got to do with it?

LT.-COLONEL (to the JOURNALIST): Khimki-Kovrino.

SON (aggressively to the CRITIC): In all events, Nikolai Aleksandrovich is totally irrelevant here.

CRITIC (aggressively to the SON): No, it's Aleksandr Nikolayevich who's totally irrelevant.

SON: Nikolai Aleksandrovich, Nikolai Aleksandrovich!

CRITIC: Aleksandr Nikolayevich, Aleksandr Nikolayevich!

SON (furiously): Aleksandr Aleksandrovich!

CRITIC (furiously): Nikolai Nikolayevich!

(The HOSTESS, smiling politely and at a loss for words, parts them silently like boxers in a ring.)

JOURNALIST (to the LT.-COLONEL): It's a long way out though. What are they doing with your old building — pulling it down?

SON (to the CRITIC): Besides, the play's disgustingly anti-semitic. Two Jews are raped in it.

CRITIC: I beg your pardon, but that's nonsense. Just because the author depicts Jews being raped doesn't mean he's an anti-semite! On the contrary, he's defending the Jews.

SON: But in his play a Jew rapes a Jew.

CRITIC: Surely you noticed that the Jew who raped the Jew was himself raped afterwards. And anyway, how can the author be an anti-semite — he's a Jew himself.

LT-.COLONEL (to the JOURNALIST): No, I joined a co-operative.

LADY (to the CRITIC): Is he really Jewish? I thought his wife was Jewish and he himself was Russian.

CRITIC: No, he's a Jew. It's his wife who is Russian in fact.

SON: No, it's not his wife but his mother who is Russian, so that he's not completely Jewish.

DAUGHTER: I think you've got it

wrong. It's his father who is Russian and his mother's Jewish.

JOURNALIST (to the LT.-COLONEL): How many rooms have you got?

LADY (to the DAUGHTER): I knew his mother — she's not Jewish at all. It's his wife's mother who is Jewish.

CRITIC: You think she's Jewish? You're mistaken — it's her husband who's Jewish.

SON: No, not the husband, the wife.

LT.-COLONEL (to the JOURNALIST): Two rooms. There are three of us — my mother, myself and my wife.

HOSTESS (tentatively): The playwright's wife or his father's?

SON: The playwright's wife.

DAUGHTER: The father's wife.

CRITIC: They're getting you in a muddle. In actual fact, we're not talking about the wife, but the husband.

JOURNALIST (to the LT.-COLONEL): What kind of building is it — concrete-panelled or brick?

HOSTESS: How interesting! Whose husband?

CRTIC: The playwright's wife's husband.

LADY: The father's wife's husband.

LT.-COLONEL (to the JOURNALIST): Panel-built. We're on the fourth floor.

HOSTESS (tentatively): And are they Russian or Jewish?

CRITIC: Jewish.

LADY: No, Russian.

CRITIC: Jewish, Jewish.

LADY: Russian, Russian!

CRITIC (furiously): Jewish!

LADY (furiously): Russian!

HOSTESS (politely): Ah, now I see: they are Russian Jews.

JOURNALIST (to the LT.-COLONEL): Is there a lift?

LADY (to the CRITIC): Did you notice that there wasn't a single female part in the play?

CRITIC: Yes, that's true. What could it mean?

LADY: It looks very much as though there's something perverse in his relationships with women.

DAUGHTER: Unnatural, anyway.

LT.-COLONEL (to the JOURNALIST): There's no lift — it's a five-storey building.

LADY (to the DAUGHTER): I think he's impotent.

DAUGHTER: Homosexual you mean.

LADY (triumphantly): I've got absolute proof of his impotence.

DAUGHTER (triumphantly): And I've got absolute proof of his homsexuality.

SON (to the LADY): What proof?

JOURNALIST (to the LT.-COLONEL): How high are the ceilings?

LADY: He had a friend of mine over to his place and all he asked her to do was strip and walk up and down in front of him.

DAUGHTER: And did she?

LADY: Yes, poor thing. He gave her a boys' brigade drum and ordered her to beat it and sing 'May the sun always shine!'

HOSTESS: How dreadful!

LT.-COLONEL (to the JOURNALIST): Unfortunately, they're low. And the sound-proofing is poor.

LADY: Well, the upstairs neighbours started banging on the floor, as it was already late and the drumming was stopping them sleeping. So she left his place without anything to show for it.

CRITIC (to the DAUGHTER): And what about your proof?

DAUGHTER: To look at, Uncle Jack's a big, tough man, but I'm told that once he got drunk at a party and ran round the room shouting 'I'm a girl, I'm a girl!' — and then made pretty obvious advances to a male acquaintance of mine.

HOSTESS: How dreadful!

JOURNALIST (to the LT.-COLONEL):

And what did you pay per square yard?

CRITIC (to the DAUGHTER): And what did he say?

DAUGHTER (identifying proudly with her friend): Naturally he refused.

LADY: In that case, it doesn't prove anything.

DAUGHTER: And neither does your story, since your friend left. If she'd gone on beating the drum another half hour, everything would have turned out all right.

LT.-COLONEL (to the JOURNALIST): A hundred and fifty.

LADY (aggressively to the DAUGHTER): Everything wouldn't have turned out all right — he's impotent.

DAUGHTER (aggressively to the LADY): No he's not, he's homosexual.

LADY: Impotent, impotent!

DAUGHTER: Homosexual, homsexual!

LADY (furiously): Impotent!

DAUGHTER (furiously): Homosexual!

HOSTESS (politely): Probably he's impotent, because he's a passive homosexual.

JOURNALIST (to the LT.-COLONEL): That's nothing. Has it got a separate bathroom and toilet?

GUEST (plucking up courage): Where did he get the drum from?

(Everyone looks at the GUEST.)

HOSTESS (amazed): Don't you know?! As well as being a playwright, Uncle Jack's a fine musician, and his place is full of musical instruments. Besides the drums, he plays the balalaika, french horn, accordion and clavichord. And recently he took up the trombone.

GUEST: How marvellous! And I don't know any instrument at all.

LT.-COLONEL (to the JOURNALIST): Unfortunately, the bathroom and toilet are combined.

DAUGHTER (to the GUEST): You don't know anything — full stop. I don't suppose you even know how to kiss.

(The GUEST retires into his shell, mortified.)

HOSTESS (to all): Excuse me a moment, I'll give him a ring and find out what's keeping him so long. (She goes.)

CRITIC (trying to bolster up the GUEST): There's no need to despair. Wisdom comes with age. Only don't forget, you have to work hard so as to develop your natural capabilities.

JOURNALIST (to the LT.-COLONEL): How long is the guarantee — a hundred years?

LADY (to the CRITIC): That's quite true. When I was young, for instance, it was discovered that I had an excellent voice, a coloratura soprano. I wanted to study and become a singer, but what with a family and children to raise there was no time for studies so that was the end of that.

LT.-COLONEL (to the JOURNALIST): Only fifty. But that's long enough for us. (He starts thinking about life.)

JOURNALIST: Yes, that's long enough for us. (He starts thinking about life.)

CRITIC (to the LADY): In my youth I was very gifted in painting. Everyone urged me to study, but those were hard times, I had to go out to work — and today I couldn't even hold a brush straight.

LT.-COLONEL (shyly): Nowadays, you don't have to know anything to paint pictures.

CRITIC (cautiously): How do you mean?

LT.-COLONEL (shyly): I read in the papers that in America they hang a shovel or dustbin on a chain and call it a picture.

CRITIC (shocked): Impossible!

LADY: Yes, that's perfectly true. I read about it in the *Literary Gazette*. It's called pop-art.

CRITIC (calmly): Oh, pop-art.

(Enter the HOSTESS.)

ALL: Well?

HOSTESS (solemnly): He asks you to excuse him for being so late. He'll be here in five minutes.

CRITIC: Excellent! (To the HOSTESS:) We're talking about pop-art.

HOSTESS (politely): How interesting! What's that?

LADY: It's a new trend in American art. The very latest.

DAUGHTER: You're mixing up pop-art and op-art. The latest trend is op-art.

LADY: I'm not mixing them up at all! Op-art is op-art and pop-art is pop-art.

CRITIC: No, no, op-art and pop-art are the same thing.

SON: That's entirely wrong. Pop-art is a branch of op-art.

DAUGHTER: You're mistaken. Op-art is a branch of pop-art.

LADY: You don't know what you're talking about. First came op-art and then pop-art, a kind of avant-garde op-art.

DAUGHTER: It's you who don't know what you're talking about. First came pop-art, and op-art appeared only after that, a kind of avant-garde pop-art.

CRITIC: You're getting confused by the terminology. Op-art is another name for pop-art.

SON: No, it's pop-art that's another name of op-art.

LADY (aggressively to the DAUGHTER): First came op-art.

DAUGHTER (aggressively to the LADY): First came pop-art.

CRITIC (aggressively to the SON): Op-art is another name.

SON (aggressively to the CRITIC): Pop-art is another name.

LADY: Op-art, op-art!

DAUGHTER: Pop-art, pop-art!

CRITIC: For pop-art!

SON: For op-art!

LADY (furiously): Op!

DAUGHTER (furiously): Pop!

(They somersault.)

CRITIC (furiously): Op!

SON (furiously): Pop!

HOSTESS (politely): A fascinating trend.

ALL: What is?

HOSTESS (confused): Pop-art. (Quickly.) And op-art too.

JOURNALIST (authoritatively): Both these trends are equally alien to us.

SON: But they're probably not alien to the Americans.

JOURNALIST: Not to snobs. To the ordinary American, the farmer or worker, they're just as alien.

SON: I shouldn't think the ordinary American could care less about art anyway.

JOURNALIST: That's because he has his work cut out making enough to feed and clothe himself and his family.

LADY: But American workers aren't so badly off.

DAUGHTER: Ordinary American women dress far better than us.

JOURNALIST: What gives you that idea?

DAUGHTER: I know, for instance, that the ordinary American woman's wardrobe contains a winter overcoat with fur trimmings . . .

JOURNALIST (interrupting her): Or without them . . .

(They all turn on the JOURNALIST.)

CRITIC: A spring coat . . .

LADY (filling in the details): Sometimes with a detachable lining . . .

SON: A raincoat . . .

LT.-COLONEL: Five house dresses . . .

GUEST: Three costumes . . .

DAUGHTER: Three skirts . . .

CRITIC: Six blouses . . .

LADY: Three jerseys or cardigans . . .

SON: Six slips . . .

LT.-COLONEL: Two under-skirts . . .

HOSTESS: Five night-dresses . . .

GUEST: Eight pairs of panties . . .

DAUGHTER: Five bodices . . .

CRITIC: Two corsets or suspender belts . . .

LADY: Two dressing-gowns . . .

SON: Six pairs of nylon stockings . . .

LT.-COLONEL: Two pairs of sports socks . . .

HOSTESS: Three pairs of gloves . . .

GUEST: A swimming suit . . .

DAUGHTER: Three pairs of shorts . . .

CRITIC: A pair of slacks . . .

LADY: A sports outfit . . .

(They crowd round the JOURNALIST. A ring.)

JOURNALIST (softly): And various subsidiary toilet articles.

(Another ring.)

HOSTESS: At last!

(The HOSTESS hurries out into the hall. The LADY and the DAUGHTER start making themselves up. A brief, muffled conversation off-stage. A woman who looks a bit of a trouble-maker enters with the HOSTESS. General bewilderment.)

ALL: Well?

HOSTESS (disappointed): Our public-spirited house committee activist has just dropped in. (To the ACTIVIST:) What is it you want, dear?

ACTIVIST (fervently): Comrades! The editorial board of our wall newspaper *For a Communist Life* is calling for contributions systematically analysing how the rules of socialist living are being observed in the block. Let us discuss the questions of the struggle against hooliganism, foul language, drunkenness, squabbling and all those things that disturb our daily lives, our work and our rest. Your articles will help the house committee to eliminate specific defects and, above all, will facilitate the establishment of new communist relations between tenants. Comrades, write about the good people living in your flats, about their good deeds! Place your contributions in the contribution box!

(Prolonged applause turning into an ovation. All rise. Cries resound: 'Glory to the house committee!', 'Long live our wall newspaper!', 'Hurrah!' Gradually all fall silent.)

JOURNALIST: It's high time our wall press attacked all the things that disturb our daily lives, our work and our rest.

HOSTESS (politely): Yes, high time. Some dreadful things are happening. You simply wouldn't believe some of the outrageous things I've heard.

LADY (heatedly): Heard! I myself was actually present when citizen Ivanov I. I., born 1930, domicile Khimki-Khovrino, block 1, house 2, building 3, flat 4, works superintendent at no. 5 building department, used obscene language in the trolleybus saloon, importuned passengers and paid no attention to the rebukes that were made. He was reported for it.

DAUGHTER (anxious to get her bit in): Recently I saw something in a restaurant that was absolutely shocking. Citizen Petrov P. P., born 1931, domicile Khoroshevo-Mnevniki, block 6, house 7, building 8, flat 9, foreman at no. 10 hairdressing saloon, caused a disturbance, insulting the civic dignity of the customers. Was sent to the sobering station.

SON: How can one really talk of mass culture when things like this happen under one's very eyes: citizen Sidorov S. S., born 1932, domicile Belyaevo-Bogorodskoye, block 11, house 12, building 13, flat 14, unemployed, consumed alcoholic spirits in his place of residence. He was sentenced to five days.

CRITIC: You're right. Things often get completely out of hand. For instance, citizen Semyonov S. S., born 1933, domicile Phili-Mazilovo, block 15, house 16, building 17, flat 18, loader at no. 19 motor depot, loitered about aimlessly on the station platform in a state of extreme intoxication. Administrative proceedings were taken against him.

LT.-COLONEL (resentfully): He was lucky.

HOSTESS: Anyway, it's a good thing proceedings *were* taken against him; sometimes people get off scot-free. A month ago, a flat was burgled in the building and the thieves haven't been caught to this day. They say the case has been closed.

ACTIVIST (persuasively): But why only look on the seamy side when there's so much good around. Only yesterday they televised a conversation with the foreman of the Moscow ship-repair works' diesel section. He spoke of his works comrades with especial pride. And do you know what he particularly praised in them?

ALL (their interest aroused): What?

ACTIVIST: Their desire to learn. Nearly all the diesel workers study. And when people find the energy to sit down over their books after a hard day's work, so as to know more the next day and be able to work better — it's a tribute to their moral sense and their public spiritedness!

JOURNALIST: And one can find a thousand similar cases!

LADY (enraptured): A thousand?! That's almost a million!

JOURNALIST (modestly): Yes, almost.

CRITIC (critically): All the same, a thousand is less than a million.

JOURNALIST (displeased): Yes, a little less.

HOSTESS (sadly): Poor lads though, it must be very hard to work and study all the time. It's enough to drive you out of your mind!

(They protest one after another, trying to make the HOSTESS see things differently.)

CRITIC: But why? You know the saying, it's dogged wins.

LADY: Work and study catches the worm.

LT.-COLONEL: Work and study make you strong and ruddy.

ACTIVIST: Work and study go hand in hand.

JOURNALIST: He who loves to work does not study shirk.

DAUGHTER: He whose companion's a book shines also at work.

SON: Work is the source of creation, books are the source of information.

CRITIC (to the LADY): By the way, there's a large selection of books on every subject in no. 20 bookshop.

LADY (to the CRITIC): There's also a large selection of prints, reproductions, postcards and albums.

LT.-COLONEL (to the ACTIVIST): In no. 21 commission shop* they take women's shoes on commission.

ACTIVIST (to the LT.-COLONEL): Shoes are the best gift for a woman.

JOURNALIST (to the HOSTESS): In no. 22 polyclinic of the department of self-supporting medical institutions, patients are admitted by professors and consultants.

HOSTESS (to the JOURNALIST): A daily list of appointments is drawn up.

SON (to the DAUGHTER): In no. 23 hairdressing and barber's establishment the collective of communist labour attends to you.

DAUGHTER (to the SON): There are men's and women's departments.

CRITIC (to the LADY): No. 24 taxi depot is offering employment to second and third class drivers.

LT.-COLONEL (to the ACTIVIST): The permanent exhibition of economic achievements encourages the new, the advanced and the progressive.

LADY (to the CRITIC): The taxi is the most convenient form of transport.

ACTIVIST (to the LT.-COLONEL): No. 25 dumpling eating house has been opened in the grounds of the exhibition.

JOURNALIST (to the HOSTESS): The Moscow Canal is one of the glorious

*A shop where second-hand goods are sold on commission.

achievements of our epoch.

SON (to the DAUGHTER): No. 26 post-office takes subscriptions to magazines and newspapers.

HOSTESS (to JOURNALIST): A river boat trip is the best form of relaxation.

DAUGHTER (to the SON): The newspaper is not only a collective agitator and propagandist, but also a collective organiser.*

CRITIC (to the LADY): No. 27 training shop is inviting students to join its salesmanship courses.

LT.-COLONEL (to the ACTIVIST): The great science of chemistry provides the people with new commodities.

JOURNALIST (to the HOSTESS): The staff of no. 28 milk-bar has taken part in a public review of the work of the enterprise.

SON (to the DAUGHTER): A junior nurse is required for no. 29 amalgamated maternity consultation clinic attached to no. 30 maternity home.

LADY (to the CRITIC): The labour force recruiter's office is open between the hours of 31 and 32 daily.

ACTIVIST (to LT.-COLONEL): No. 33 tailor's shop attached to no. 34 factory is offering to repair ladders in stockings.

HOSTESS (to the JOURNALIST): No. 35 reception point at no. 36 food store will buy empties in any quantity.

DAUGHTER (to the SON): Payments for beer to be made at counters no. 37, 38, 39 . . .

CRITIC (following on): 40, 41, 42 . . .

LADY: 43, 44, 45 . . .

LT.-COLONEL: 46, 47, 48 . . .

ACTIVIST: 49, 50, 51 . . .

JOURNALIST: 52, 53, 54 . . .

HOSTESS: 55, 56, 57 . . .

SON: 58, 59, 60 . . .

DAUGHTER: And 61. Plates and dishes are taken only in exchange.

*This is a quotation from Lenin.

GUEST (plucking up courage): Number one million one thousand and sixty two electrical assembly department . . .

CRITIC (interrupting the GUEST belligerently): How can you talk like that! Electricity's a boon; you should have proper respect for it!

LADY (belligerently to the GUEST): Remember that one kilowatt-hour is enough to bake a hundred loaves of bread!

LT.-COLONEL (belligerently to the GUEST): Or to produce ten kilograms of cement!

ACTIVIST (belligerently to the GUEST): Or to stitch a pair of boots.

(They turn on the GUEST one after another.)

JOURNALIST: Have your shoes repaired in time!

HOSTESS: All comments and remarks to be entered in the book provided for that purpose!

SON: In case of a gas leak turn off the tap!

DAUGHTER: Buy goods on credit!

CRITIC: Eat tinned fish!

LADY: Take care when passing standing vehicles!

LT.-COLONEL: Pay the correct fare!

ACTIVIST: Struggle to raise the cultural level of life!

JOURNALIST: Collect non-ferrous metal scrap!

HOSTESS: Buy lottery tickets!

SON: Read magazines, newspapers, books!

DAUGHTER: Drink tomato juice!

CRITIC: Fly by plane!

LADY: Eliminate flies!

LT.-COLONEL (clicking his heels in excitement): Come and buy, come and buy, they're juicy and sweet!

GUEST (retreating, scrambles onto a chair, snatches a pair of panties from the line and flourishes them like a flag. The whole company advances

(Continuing to shout, they tie up the
GUEST and get more and more

entangled in the string themselves as the ball unwinds.)

CRITIC: Comrade Sidorov's system!

LADY: Ivan Ivanovich arse!

LT.-COLONEL: Nekrasov's tradition!

ACTIVIST: May the sun always shine!

JOURNALIST: A thousand is less than a million.

HOSTESS: Tossing your head like a horse.

SON: Sent to the sobering station!

DAUGHTER: Trotskyists are onanists!

CRITIC: Apotheosis of good!

LADY: Annihilate flies!

LT.-COLONEL: Civic dignity!

ACTIVIST: Maoists are optimists!

JOURNALIST: I'm a girl, I'm a girl!

HOSTESS: Centrists are pederasts!

SON: Almost like Ionesco!

DAUGHTER: A collective agitator!

CRITIC: On sale!

LADY: Revisionists are masochists!

LT.-COLONEL: Permanent exhibition of achievements!

ACTIVIST: Intellectuals are impotent!

JOURNALIST: He is in me and I am in space!

HOSTESS: All politics is paralytics!

SON: Labour force recruiter!

DAUGHTER: Forced labour recruiter!

CRITIC: Long enough for us!

LADY: Desire to learn.

LT.-COLONEL: The drum and trombone!

ACTIVIST: Church mass!

JOURNALIST: Choc mousse!

(A loud ring. Exit the HOSTESS, trailing the string behind her. They are all more or less tangled up in it. There is string round the legs of the chairs and table and the pictures on the wall. They all dash round the room except for the GUEST who is securely tied.)

SON: Grocery-gastronome!

DAUGHTER: Haberdashery-knitwear!

CRITIC: Cigarettes-tobacco!

LADY: Vegetables-fruit!

LT.-COLONEL: China-pottery!

ACTIVIST: Meat-fish!

JOURNALIST: Juices-waters!

SON: Left! (He flings himself to the left.)

DAUGHTER: Right! (She flings herself to the right.)

CRITIC: Right!

LADY: Left!

LT.-COLONEL: Right!

ACTIVIST: Left!

JOURNALIST: Left!

SON: Right!

(The HOSTESS returns entangled in string.)

HOSTESS (solemnly): Uncle Jack has arrived!

(The sounds of a drum getting louder. It could be the playwright's footsteps down the corridor, or the guests' hearts beating in eager anticipation. The trussed-up GUEST suddenly comes to life and cries out in horror. The furniture topples over, the paintings drop off the wall, the SON has leapt up and thrown string over the chandelier which sways threateningly. Some of the guests fall to the floor, the rest caper about the room, dragging along those who have fallen. They have got caught up in the sheets hanging on the line and look like ghosts.)

ALL:
He's come, he's come! Ha-ha-ha-ha!
We are the fowl's offspring!
He's come, he's come! Ha-ha-ha-ha!
We don't live in the woods for nothing!

(The drumbeat grows louder. The GUEST screams. They all dash around the stage. The chandelier falls. At this point, the scenery collapses to the uproarious Homeric laughter of the audience. This is the end of the play. The curtain falls.)

Moscow 1964

As well as Theatrescripts like this book, **Eyre Methuen** publish a wide range of modern plays and theatre books. Authors include Jean Anouilh, John Arden, Brendan Behan, Edward Bond, Bertolt Brecht, Howard Brenton, Shelagh Delaney, Max Frisch, Simon Gray, Peter Handke, David Mercer, Joe Orton, Harold Pinter, Stephen Poliakoff and Wole Soyinka, as well as Buchner, Gogol, Gorky, Ibsen, Jarry, Synge and Oscar Wilde.

If you would like to receive regular information about these and other Eyre Methuen drama books, please write to The Marketing Department, Eyre Methuen Ltd, North Way, Andover Hampshire. Please say if you would particularly like to be kept informed about future Theatrescripts.